THE RINGING EAR

The

Ringing Ear

BLACK POETS LEAN SOUTH

EDITED BY NIKKY FINNEY

The University of Georgia Press | Athens & London

Credits for previously published poems appear on pages
379–83 and constitute an extension of this copyright page.

Published by The University of Georgia Press
Athens, Georgia 30602
© 2007 by Cave Canem Foundation, Inc.
All rights reserved
Set in 10/14 Minion by BookComp, Inc.
Printed and bound by Sheridan Books

The paper in this book meets the guidelines for
permanence and durability of the Committee on
Production Guidelines for Book Longevity of the
Council on Library Resources.

Printed in the United States of America
11 10 09 08 07   C   5 4 3 2 1
11 10 09 08 07   P   5 4 3 2 1

Library of Congress Cataloging-in-Publication Data

The ringing ear : Black poets lean south / edited by
Nikky Finney.
          p.   cm.
ISBN-13: 978-0-8203-2925-3 (alk. paper)
ISBN-10: 0-8203-2925-8 (alk. paper)
ISBN-13: 978-0-8203-2926-0 (pbk. : alk. paper)
ISBN-10: 0-8203-2926-6 (pbk. : alk. paper)
1. American poetry–African American authors. 2. American
poetry–Southern States. 3. African Americans–Poetry.
4. Southern States–Poetry. 5. American poetry–21st century.
I. Finney, Nikky. II. Cave Canem (Organization)
PS591.N4R56 2007
811'.6080896073–dc22
2006031013

British Library Cataloging-in-Publication Data available

*For the 250 years of Black poetic genius we follow, represent,
and steadily beckon, and for the unmoored
but unsinkable of New Orleans*

Say the moment crossing over rights the left
Say the moment crossing over is the ringing ear writing
Say the moment crossing over ends hear

—Forrest Hamer

CONTENTS

Swimming, Childhood, and Other Thunders:
Don't Get Your Hot Hair Wet or Your Good Shoes Dirty

The Echo and Din of Place: Turn in by the Silver Queen
and Double Twisted Pine

The Twenty-first-Century Southern Riff and Shout:
Modern Lullabies for Planet Octavia

ACKNOWLEDGMENTS

Kendra Hamilton and Lenard Moore—for giving birth to the idea for this book and for pulling the first pages through the slippery canal—

Carolyn Micklem—for your foundational faith in this collection, for years of steering and sailing the Cave Canem steamship into so many ports, for speaking your mind and encouraging with all your might—

Dante Micheaux—for your daily editorial largesse. Your diligent, mindful work, the essential matter and the minutiae, now etched on the back and front of every page herein—

The Ford Foundation—for providing shingle and shade to Cave Canem, worthy wondrous Black poetry planet—

Lucille Clifton—for waiting at the tiny window to your front door for me to get out of the car, as I nervously spilled microphone and tape player nearly into the street, for inviting me into your home, for sharing three hours of treasured word and laughter, spread between the chips, mints, and quiet, quirky, solitary-girl recognition—

The University of Georgia Press—for championing our words out into the world—

HEIRLOOMS AND INTRODUCTIONS: THE POET IS THE TRUMPET OF THE WORLD

June 2000: I step outside the Detroit airport terminal and see it, a small cardboard sign in a shuttle bus window: *Cave Canem.* My hand and arm rise into the air as if my name has been called. I am present and answering. I walk toward the bus. The doors open. Inside, striated voices are buzzing. The sound of honey is everywhere. Their smiles, hellos, whispers, and open journal books surround me. I choose a seat. There are twenty or so other Black poets on the bus so far. We will wait for another plane to land before we head to the site. The bus door opens. Another poet enters and takes her seat. Soon the bus leaves the airport, headed to the private grounds of Cranbrook Academy just outside of Detroit.

Cranbrook has been rented for the fifth annual Cave Canem summer writing workshop. There is no permanent home place for Black poets and their work, not yet. Cranbrook is where everyone on the bus and others will spend one week together this summer working on poetry. We have not flown, driven, bused, or hailed our trains here to work on the ever popular, ever talked about novels, short stories, scripts, or memoirs. We have arrived with our precious musically compressed words. Poetry. Verse. Poesy. The grace of literature.

I don't know anybody on the bus, and yet I know everybody.

As a girl, I knew no others like me, other girls who fell in love with paper and pencils, like some girls fell in love with Easy-Bake ovens and dolls. As a young woman I never met another who would have walked twenty country miles, in bad shoes, in a lightning storm, just to hear Margaret Walker read "For My People" on a stage somewhere, anywhere, without a micro- or megaphone. Anywhere.

As an adult, I have written three poetry books and have traveled far and wide sharing words and moments from each. I have traveled out of the country and around the world. I am a tenured professor at a state university with 25,000 students. The wet has long dried behind my ears. I have seen a thing or two in my life. But, before June 2000, I had never seen anything like the sweet phenomenon that I saw on that shuttle bus: Black poets arriving from cities and towns all over, to travel into the woods, to work on metaphor, line length, stanzas, word choice, rhythm, balance, image clarity. Never had I felt so at home. At long last, my lost tribe.

By the end of the week I was cakewalking the grounds of Cranbrook in between the workshop hours, head down in moving meditation, whispering, *I just didn't know there were so many of us alive in North America.* I wasn't talking about bald eagles. I was talking about Black poets.

After my first year as a faculty member at Cave Canem, I realized Black poets in America were not an endangered species, but we were being starved to the brink of extinction, starved and kept from each other's eyes and arms. Most of us had been encouraged to get an education. Many had been encouraged to read, read, and read some more, but many of us had also been generously warned by family and teachers to get *real* jobs and leave "childish things," like poetry, behind.

Rewind: In slavery times, a Black person caught with a pencil or book meant the loss of a hand, foot, eye, or worse. *Forward*: In modern times, Black people + America + poetry often times = a life of not being taken seriously and isolation. *But you write so well. Why not try a novel instead?* We didn't recognize each other, before the bus ride, because we had never officially met. Buses and bus rides had been known to pull Black folks together before, and to even start movements. This moment was no exception.

The first night of a Cave Canem week is the most mesmerizing of all. Black poets making each other's acquaintance for the first time. Seventy-five Black poets sitting in an elephant-size circle, nervous knee bone to nervous knee bone, smiling eye to jumping eye. Introductions. Who is faculty? Who is fellow? Who cares. Everyone has a poem up their sleeve. We sit across from and beside each other. Our eyes stare. Our minds dance. We are speechless. Uncensored. Uncut. Our chains broken for the week. Our tongues become bright red Ferraris against the warm mosquito night air. We are both free and frozen in some strange mix of floating pentameter, bright hunger, and sweet first-time recognition. *Abracadabra. We are here.*

There is nothing like being seen by the eyes of those who, without explanation, understand why you do what you do when you do it. There is nothing like not having to decode or apologize for the sweet pleasure of a word or phrase that will not let loose of your ear. *Memory*: two a.m. I walk down the hallway one quiet Cranbrook night, on the way to the bathroom in a garish grandmotherly bathrobe, and find two young poets leaning into the third page of Marilyn Nelson's Petrarchan treatise-sonnet on Emmett Till, discussing line length and enjambment, oblivious to me and my robe. *Excuse me,* I whisper. I am a well-raised southern girl. I know to apologize when I intrude, but neither poet lifts his high-beam concentrating wooly head.

There is no place on this planet, no ground, no air, no sanctuary, no wharf, no hermitage, no refuge, no time like the one week each summer when Black poets descend on an unsuspecting space and it becomes Cave Canem. Toi Derricotte and Cornelius Eady gave birth to more than an idea when visiting Italy in 1995. While inside the House of the Tragic Poet in Pompeii, they were struck by the image in a mosaic of a black dog on a broken chain and the words *Cave Canem* inscribed beneath. *Cave Canem,* Latin, means "beware of the dog." Derricotte and Eady wanted to bring Black poets of all ages, abilities, and backgrounds together under a planned and organized umbrella. They were clear that Black poets needed to lay eye and ear on each other. What these brilliant, passionate, poet-teachers pushed out, via Pompeii, was a new planet, but what they also touched was an heirloom. We have not handed down, for hundreds of years, from Miss Phillis to Miss Lucille, the firefly words of who we are, what we must do, build, and be: outlier, insider, culture seed thrower, beauty seer. Whenever Black people in twenty-first-century America forego outside permission to have what they need and push through to find a way out of no way, it is beyond visionary, it is nothing short of planetary, a truly twenty-first-century heirloom. See part 7, *Modern Lullabies for Planet Octavia.* (We miss you.)

This collection of poetry, *The Ringing Ear,* has southern leanings. Not all of us on these pages have come to or from the South by the same dirt road. We have not chosen our dark olive words from the same patch of earth. Some have come by way of birth and others have followed street musicians and urban corner preachers, dream and myth, to stand before its pine and iron gates. We who are here claim the South in what and how we hear ourselves say and do and wonder. Our South, with its ghosts and fiddles, its fine sugar waters and shine. We obey its voice in us but we are no Dixie gents and chicks. We remember the confederacy of slaves even though there are no bronze statues in any courthouse squares from Mississippi to Florida.

Over ten years have passed since Cave Canem's creation, and in North America it has become the major nexus for Black poetry. Cave Canem put out a call for Black poets with southern leanings for this collection. Those who answered the call and made the final pages have not all been a part of the Cave Canem Summer Writing Workshop. Some of those who answered were simply within earshot of other Black poets. The call went out like a beam of light, and that beam was seen by those keeping watch for it in the distance. The poems poured in. The light from their pages was blinding with that unmistakable heirloom brilliance. Some arrived with questions and qualifiers: *My daddy was born in the South, does that make me southern enough?* Or, *I've never actually been to the South, but I am haunted in my dreams every night by swamplands and/or magnolia trees. Can I send something?* Or, *I drove through Greenwood, Mississippi, once when I was fifteen. I've never forgotten or seen another road go on for so long. I have written a poem about it. May I?*

Yes, you may. Who, what, and when is southern? I am a southerner and I do not consider myself a regional anything. I consider myself a worldly woman with South Carolina at the heart of that world. For the sake of this anthology and for the ongoing debate about who is and who isn't, I looked for southern thread and fragrances. I used some of the old tropes as a starting place but not as a stop sign. I decided there would be no southern blood test. Enough of the three-quarter, one-drop, rule. The stereotypes of what some people believe a southerner is and what others believe she isn't are too one-dimensional for me. I did not want this anthology to be mired in predictable notions. The world is in constant flux; so too is the South. I know what the Mason-Dixon line represents and I know it is not a sixty-foot wall with razor wire at the top but rather a historical marker that since its construction people and culture readily cross. "Melting pot" is a loose American term. The Black community has never melted. We have marched. We have organized. We have fought. We have been shot at, fired at, and spit at. We have been abandoned on rooftops in the middle of a devastating hurricane. We have migrated away and intermarried. We have been hanged for sport. We have stayed on these shores kicking, screaming, loving, forgiving, and writing, but we have never melted into this or any other country.

I wanted exceptional poetry for this collection. I wanted a mix of old and new voices, recognizable and unrecognizable names. I wanted new windows on old worlds. New takes on old feelings. I wanted subjects—like love and sexuality—that have been around forever but rarely explored and honestly examined to have light and lift. As editor I wished to add wings to the old traditional categories of food, religion, land, memory, and family. I hoped to keep some of those old rootstock vines deep in the ground of this book but also to watch for new blooms. A poet did not have to prove his/her southern blood type to get in. A poet did have to show originality and connection to the sanguine South.

There are poets in these pages who took typewriter and pencil straight to their desire to grasp and interpret what headlines, mamas, politicians, and early twentieth-century America could and did not: Black people willing to mail their bodies to freedom, delirious Ford trucks filled with family moving South to North on a hope and two prayers, silver dimes instead of wooden nickels pushed deep inside hankies and mason jars. There are poets here whose dreams climbed inside of the fabric of the noose in 1919 and the circlet of Black bodies that dangled from trees. Read their work and they will tell you what they know, how they feel, and what they saw. The imperfect South has called us together to this campground of pages. It has called us together with its charcoal Choctaw air, its narrow-minded news, its balsam throat, its blind devotion to barbecue and authority, its great goober heart and unforgettable peach mouth. It is our Southland, where music was born of salty tears and wicked wailing weather, where dance should never be confused with the fever of feet during sacred Watchnight.

This anthology closes with a conversation I was privileged to have with Lucille Clifton near the eve of her seventieth birthday. I flew to Maryland to sit with her. I was nervous and so was she. I believe it was because we so clearly recognized each other over the phone and also in our work. I first read Lucille Clifton as a girl-poet of twenty-three, never imagining that she and I would twenty-five years later have an intimate conversation about what it means to be a Black woman poet in 2006, an heirloom moment for sure. I knew Buffalo and Depew, New York, were her homes. I knew her people had migrated from Virginia. But who knew she was a *Jeopardy!* champion! We had never met before that moment but knowing her work and witnessing her ways, I felt that her southern leanings were clear and must anchor this collection. Her fierce love for her Blackness, her tenacious independent humanity, her deep connection to her family, her huge eighteen-chambered gracious heart for her friends, her refusal to bite her tongue, ever, her sassiness, her employment of the blues, her high-lonesome succinct way of saying, the way she protects her quirky mind, her refusal to "suffer fools easily," her ease with laughter, all proved she leaned in the direction of what I knew to be southern.

The initial idea for gathering up contemporary Black poetry with southern harmonies and notes was conceived by poets Kendra Hamilton and Lenard Moore. The lovely story goes that the idea was born on yet another pleather seat ride, on yet another Cave Canem bus. Without their rich creative juices and sweat equity this book would still be a chance not taken.

The architecture of *The Ringing Ear* is built around sound. Sound is surely at the heart of poetry. Naming the seven parts helped me tremendously in establishing a collective trumpet of notes. The titles of the parts establish the foundation between the old tropes and the new, such as part 1, "Music, Food, and Work." The part subtitles lift the old world thinking up into the new, as in "Heeding the Lamentation and Roar of Things Made by Hand." The verb "heeding" helps build the bridge and adds the needed motion. The addition of the specific sound-words adds something, I hope, wondrous and sensory based. This is the kind of energy that I wanted each section divider to create for the worlds about to be revealed to the reader.

It was an absolute imperative that the title of this project be born out of the work itself. As a poet and writer, I believe in this kind of organic arrangement. *The Ringing Ear* was pulled from Forrest Hamer's masterful meditative poem "The Middle Ear." I am deeply grateful for the perfect pitch of his words being used for the greater good.

Nikky Finney
August 2006

Heeding the Lamentation and Roar
of Things Made by Hand

Dirty Rice

With bits of crawfish
the man makes me tremble.
He feeds me the tiny meat.
I taste the salt on his fingers
and want his cold gin.

At the French Market
he puts bell peppers to my nose,
presses my finger to eggplant and okra.
Back home he washes two tomatoes in the sink,
sprinkles them with salt and pepper, holds the fruit
to my lips. He says, *Bite, Cher.*

On Royal Street he teaches me to eat
oysters arranged on a plate of crushed ice,
how to spread Tabasco and horseradish on the raw flesh
and loosen my throat for the slide of muscle,
then chase with the cool yeast of a Jax.

His favorite is the dirty rice
his mama made when he was a boy.
He slices livers and gizzards, drops them in a skillet
of butter and glassy onions. The kitchen table, covered
with shrimp, is a bed of sweet craving.

Rabbit

My father said best to begin small,
with rabbits, that the shotgun's butt
should tuck in my shoulder's palette
and that God's sovereignty must
feel like spotting an eye in the thicket.

This was Granddaddy's farm,
not our subdivision's patient lawns.
We jumped cottontails from sticker bushes
to pare them to a pound
of meat. My father nested me
in his body against the recoil
that sung up my arms.

            He told me
of my great uncle who, Depression era,
loaned white townspeople venison
and preserves. Later stood off
the same ones with a gun
when they wanted his property.

This isn't a story of kindness,
he warned. Even rabbits have
distress signals at death.

. . .

To dress them: head cut, body bled,
hock joints slit, fur in fist
to strip the skin. Our whole winter.
My father's position terminated
in "fiscal rearrangements."

He said to be a good hunter one
became the target. My father dashed
gun to chest, balanced his breath
for a taste of sweet meat.

Time with Stevie Wonder in It

Winter, the empty air outside,
cold shaking its stiff tongue
announcing itself like something stone,
spit out, which is still a story
and a voice to be embraced.
Januaried movements but I hear a tune
carries me home to Lansing.

Always waiting for signs of thaw,
dark nomads getting covered by snow,
our parents would group in the long night—
tune frequencies to the Black stations
blasting out of Memphis, Nashville,
still playing what was played down South—
Ray Charles, Charles Brown, Ruth Brown, Muddy, and Wolf.

The tribal families driven north
to neighborhoods stacked like boxes—
to work the auto plants was progress,
to pour steel would buy a car
to drive hope further on down the road.
How could you touch, hear,
or be alive; how could anybody

. . .

wearing our habits, quiet Protestant
monad heads aimed up to some future?
This was our religion—
buy at J.C. Penney and Woolworth's,
work at Diamond Reo, Oldsmobile, Fisher Body.
On Fridays drink, dance, and try to forget
the perverse comfort of huddling in

what was done to survive (the hollow
auto, rule following). How could we not
"turn the head / pretend not to see?"
This is what we saw: hope screwed
to steel flesh, this was machine city
and the wind through it—neutral
to an extent, private, and above all

perfectly European language
in which we could not touch, hear,
or be alive. How could anybody
be singing "Fingertips?" Little Stevie
Wonder on my crystal, 1963.
Blind boy comes to go to school,
the air waves politely segregated.

———————

If this were just a poem,
there would be a timelessness—
the punchclock Midwest would go on
ticking, the intervals between ticks
metaphor for the gap in our lives
and in the language which would not
carry itself beyond indifferent

• • •

consequences. The beauty of the word,
though, is the difference between language
and the telling made through use.
Dance Motown on his lip, he slips
these radio tracks across the synapse
of snow. The crystals show
a future happening with you in it.

Night Shift/Day Shift

The trolleys click
like metronomes

measuring
the unconcealed prayers
of your mother
or mine; from the window
I smell their talcum
and see their houses,
calm and folded
Buddhas on fat haunches,
curtains waving white
as bridal gloves.

Bending, washing,
standing and ironing
swing the breasts
like a rosary,
planting secret screams
deep in their mysterious laps,
the soft sides of their arms
collecting steam
and soap.

• • •

A wide-skirted
black dance
rustles cloth in a cedar chest;
the reverent
feet of midwives
carry the sound.

A pendulum
of female motion
keeps the coin jar full.

Don't Know What Love Is

My mother can't recall the exact
infamous year but Mama does know
that she and her friends were teenagers
when they sneaked out to an official joint
in the middle of the woods to listen
to Dinah Washington sing their favorite
love song. They wanted to dance together
so close they'd be standing behind
each other but Mama says, *Dinah showed*
up late and acted ugly and on top of
that she didn't want to sing the song.
This is supposed to be the story of Mama's
blues and how she threw good money
after bad but this is South Georgia
and Dinah's standing in high heels on a Jim
Crow stage two feet off the ground.
She's sniffing the perfume of homemade
cigarettes, chitlin plates, hair grease one
grade above Vaseline, and the premature
funk wafting up from the rowdy kids
with no home training. Can't even pee
straight much less recognize a silver lamé
dress. All they know to do is demand
one song because they risked a certain
butt whipping to be in this joint, in these woods.
Dinah won't sing it, though.
She just won't sing the song.
I'm an evil gal, she hollers out instead.
Don't you bother with me!

Joe Chappel's Foot Log Bottom Blues, 1952

I left that bottle
at the Blue Moon.
Emptied the bottle
at the Blue Moon.
And I'm gon see
my woman soon.

She lives in a shack with
a chicken yard and coop.
Got to be quiet—don't wake
them hens sleep in the coop.
To get in that shack gon have to
bow, scrape, and stoop.
Oh, I say I'm gon have
to bow, scrape, and stoop.

I need a taste more—gon stop
by Bobby's for a sip.
Needed a taste more so
stopped by Bobby's for a sip.
Now, Lord, it's done come up
a cloud mighty quick.

• • •

Clouds done moved in quick
and filled up this room.
Clouds done come and covered up
the stars and moon;
I expect, it's gon come down
a rain awful soon.

Got to cross Ten Yard Branch
to the other side.
Got to cross the branch
to the Choiceville side.
I just tripped over a root
and damn near died.

Here I am stumbling—
drunk off some liquor.
I say, I'm stumbling drunk
from stump liquor.
Going to see my woman—
Lord, all we do is bicker.

My troubles fill a pail faster
than this rain coming down.
Said, troubles overflow faster
than rain coming down.
Lord, lightning shined them raindrops
like gems in your crown.
Lord, she a good and beautiful woman
like a jewel in your crown.

These foot logs getting slapped
and kissed by the rising branch.
I said, foot logs kissed
and slapped by the rising branch.
Lord, hope I can get across
and she lift that latch.

Glutton

I could barely lift the slop buckets
we kept in the house
on account of stray dogs
and bored teenagers

After collecting contributions
from neighbors in exchange for
false promises
of a foot or a ham
come Christmas
I would ride in the back
of a pickup truck with the slop
all the way to Davistown
where Mamma's second husband
housed a litter of pigs

They squealed and gobbled down
corn cobs, potato peelings
apple cores, moldy bread, chicken bones
hard cheese, orange rinds and burnt toast

Like him
they didn't need to hear Mamma say amen
to start eating
and they wouldn't stop
until everything was gone

. . .

Watching them grow fat and slow
and mean
didn't increase my appetite
for pork chops, bacon or fathers

I was too soft
to be a real farmer, he said
and I'd better keep my head
in them books
or learn to starve
when I became a man

back in blues

next time
i'll be a blues singer
        a body encased in sequins
        gardenia swirls
        and thunderbird in my glass

won't tell you to love me
just fuck you voiceless
        blues a song up out my gravel
lined throat cry you a note about
how i wish i never met you
        then beg you to stay

velvet   my voice ain't
velvet   just rock and moan
broken   dismelody

can't be
pretty   cause
pretty   be yella

yella dresses
yella gals
yella lips
sipping yella lemonade

shaded from alabama
sunshine   all made up for soprano solos
and easter church services   yea

Fish

You don't care bout no fish.

But these sisters
in floral housedresses
and can'tgetnoblacker
straw hats

would cast
away Saturday
with cane poles
and dough bait.

Keeping every fish
to fry and fellowship
with white bread
and spaghetti.

And putting
the evil eye
on any child
bold enough

to throw
rocks
in their
good water.

• • •

They had lived all week
in other folks' kitchens
with their souls tied
behind their backs.

red onion hoodoo

see gul
dis how you keep him

muh deah says
gap smiled   stirs with one hand   holds a bad hip with the other
     winks at paw paw

gotta have three day ol corn bread fo da dressin
     lotsa lotsa butter

chopped gizzards
stewing in broth
all afternoon

collards from da garden
     hocks and some garlic

     see da hoodoo be in da root child
pull a red onion up from the earth
color tween plum and the seed of a peach

take yo time
     dice it right
     dice it fine

. . .

so the fragrance
jigs around the house
like chilluns on saturday nights grindin
sweatin holes in da walls

get da smell
in da cracks of da foundation
behind da wallpaper
in da curtains

      throw some in da greens
            in da dressin

      she whirls a wooden spoon
      over a thinning white afro
shimmies across buckled
      linoleum floor

young thangs
young thangs
don't know how to keep a man home
with one flick of dey wrist

have him tugging apron
strings when da oven door
come down
          before the supper bell rings

Night Work

In the changeling air before morning
they are silhouettes. Dark ones
with the duskiness of predawn on them
and the shading of dust and sweat.
Busying themselves in buildings,
on scaffolds, and on the black
washed pavements, they are phantoms
of the city—guardians of parking lots
and lobby desks, tollbooths, meters,
the all-nights and delivery trucks.
At bus stops they are sentinels
and the drivers. Launderers and cleaners
readying the offices and untidy houses
of privilege. Cooks heaping up meals
for the well fed, the disabled, or the indifferent.
Trash-takers, making room for more.
Nurses, eternally watching.

• • •

When my mother, starting the stove
at 5 a.m., looked out the window, she saw
her father, days after his funeral.
Had he come back to the field
and the plowing left undone when
the chain snapped and struck him,
knotting his throat into pain
and its aftershock of silence?
Did he return to reclaim the work
like a part of himself unfulfilled
and his story untold?
He is with us still, she said
to the inchoate brightness.
He is there even now.

Spirits are much the same in those
uncensored hours—flitting dim figures,
half-remembered apparitions, whose industry
renews and undergirds our own.
They are our counterparts: the whispering
echo of that other turning
as we turn in bed, the sigh that heaves
in the wake of some unseen act. In the darkness,
where a cycle of making and unmaking unfolds.
If anything could help us believe in
their benign presence, it is the workers,
perpetual as stars, a collective
of eyes and hands, conjuring.

YVONNE JACKSON

Doing Hair

It was hair
the same stuff we all got.
thick. thin. short. nappy. wavy. long.
We all got a cap of it of some size.

This child
the way she carried on.
Raising up, pulling against the comb.
I called her "tender headed."

It was only hair
not hard choices
like whether to pay
your man's bail
again, what to do
with that oldest gal
who won't keep her knees closed.

Hair is simple. wash. comb. straighten.
I tell mothers this when they come with confessions
of magazine clippings. Some boom out their wants
for the whole room to hear
but they palm the clipping, damp and fading.
"This is what I want."

. . .

This ain't no temple, that's grease
not incense.
That smoke is real
hair burning
a part human sacrifice.

I lay on heat, not hands
untangle confusion
make the crooked straight.
Pull simpering little girls
up to their full height.
A little fire on the head is a small thing.
Just hair.

I give them practice
in this knowing
every other Saturday
in my den turned beauty parlor,
I scald the willfulness
of kinks, curls, ringlets
out of the tender,
send them back to they mamas
flat and even.
Suffer the little girls.
The wild ones
who leave me half-done
whining and pointing
their lips set straight
their eyes cool iron,
long after my face
is erased by years,
these little sisters remember.

I am a licensed cosmetologist.
I make things plain.

Simmie Knox Paints Bill Clinton for the White House

for Anita

I was born in 1935 in Aliceville, Alabama, a sharecropper

During planting season
I would stand at the end of each tilled row
until I could see a picture
of what was to come—ripe bolls of cotton
held up by browning cups and stems.
At sundown I'd go back to the house
and draw the opposite of what I knew.
That's where I learned to use my hands
for work.

When I don't know you . . . I'm really feeling in the dark

My aunt asked me to paint a portrait of her father,
the first man buried in our family plot—his soaked back
bent over a horseless plow ablaze in my fingers.
I could paint my aunt twelve years after
she'd been dead because I could still see her
pushing the store-bought paper and watercolors
into my sixteen-year-old hands, telling me my gifts
were also God's—resurrection, eternal life.

. . .

but all I need is one good exposure

I took sixty pictures, even after shaking his hand.
We talked about growing up in the South
in turbulent times but remembered things
differently. I thought of Woolworth's bloodied
counters the day a college friend was dragged
from his stool. He thought of the doors, locked
and bolted after, how he had to walk twelve blocks
for candy.

We both know what it's like to be deprived of things

When he mentioned never knowing his father—
killed three months before his birth—I put my camera
down. He said his mother gambled and ran
into the strong arms of an alcoholic. Twice that man had drawn
a gun on them and hit him once with the butt of it.
I thought of my own fading mother then and finally
saw him clearly. His face creased and stained as any other
human face. I picked up my brush.

Can you imagine that?

Note: In 2004, Simmie Knox became the first black artist ever commissioned to paint
an official presidential portrait. The italicized lines are excerpts from an AP interview
with the artist.

The Boucherie

The old man who carried
the dusty shotgun
like a gold-plated trophy
unlatched the wooden pen.
The hog bolted forward
like a tractor
in a sugarcane field.
Three shots ripped through the air
and landed on tympanic membranes.

The men who laughed
took turns
stirry-ing the black iron pot
with a thick, splintered pole,
boiling the skin
in a thousand degrees
of fat.

The women who talked
sweat in the kitchen
swallowed by the smell
of organ meat and intestines,
extinguishing months of hunger
with blood-stained hands.

Catfish

1
He told her she was fat.
She had had a baby

and developed a warm
roll of lining for extra protection.

He cracked open his Bud Light
and yelled across his La-Z-Boy

recliner from the front room.

"Bring me another beer . . . will yah,
Pamela? Yah fat-ass heifer!"

She opened the ice box
and took out her husband's

fifth can of Bud Light.

2
Before dawn, he left with
his brother-in-law for Sparta Lake.

On the east end of town at the end
of red chat roads lined green with soybeans,

. . .

crawdads, water bugs, horseflies,
and cattails warn of the mud lake.

My momma tells me how her childhood
friend, Boston, fished in that same lake

when he was nine. Not knowing how
to swim, he went into the water.

He caught his fish but got tangled
in the tight, pale nylon fishin' line.

Round his body wrapped that fishin'
line and unto himself he drowned.

His darkness no competition for the lake's.

"Mustah been a big one," Momma says
they said 'cause the fish still moved

the line long after Boston stopped moving.

3
Catfish are scavengers. They spend most of their
time on a waterbed, sucking for
food. Some folks say

they are dirty, but I think they taste good if you
cook 'em right. Just peel back the skin off 'em, fillet
them up, dip 'em

in egg batter, roll 'em in seasoned cornmeal, and deep fry 'em
in the tastiest lard you can find. Serve 'em with almost

anything, but never forget the red hot sauce and white bread.
The bread helps the pale bones pass through the throat.

. . .

4
Aunt Pamela made the best fried catfish in Sparta.

At least that's what folks said. When her husband
and brother came back from fishin', everybody

came to get a piece. Deep-fried catfish, cornbread,
spaghetti, and coleslaw. After everyone ate,

us kids had one piece. Stuck in the hot kitchen,
away from the adults in the living room, we ate,

my cousins and me, all the fried cornmeal from the soak
plate covered with fish-grease-laden paper towels.

5
When my cousin Geri did the dishes,
she threw all the silver-plated forks,

knives, and spoons into the garbage can.

"It was just an accident," she said.
"I wasn't paying attention to what I was doing."

But even I began to wonder when dinner guests
were forced to eat fried catfish with their hands.

6
Everybody in Sparta worked for Sparta
Printing Plant or in the dank coal mines.

Peabody Coal was the one that all my uncles worked in.

At sunrise, my uncle Gary arrived home from
the night shift, his tin-plated-round lunch box

• • •

and coal-stained cotton jumpsuit black
from working at the bottom of a cave,

digging into a place he didn't know.

By morning, Aunt Pamela was there
with his breakfast ready and his bath done.

7
Do you know that you can only use
fish grease to fry fish and nothing else?

If you cook anything other than fish
in fish grease, it will come out tasting like fish.

Miss Look's Dream (Miss Look)

Miss Look:
The best part of my brother
Is the best part of my heart.

Can I offer a bit of advice?
I am walking with my dead brother
I am dreaming on a train
We are in our favorite place, the slave cemetery,
The soil springs to our step and moss itches our nose,

This is our quiet. Africa lies under our feet.
I know this not from the school, but from
My brother, who forms the word in his mouth
Like the pastor says *God*, or the cracker says *Nigger*:
Like he owns it. All the flowers in this plot feed

On the dust of kings, princes, queens, he says.
And he laughs. One part honey, one part curse,
One part train whistle steaming through a crossing.
I nod my head in agreement to his features,
The clever music he speaks.

How can he hold so much, I worry.
He has given me the names of things
And in my Sunday-school heart, I picture Adam
Painting the peacocks' feathers for his bride.
Go see the world, he suggests,

. . .

I am rolling back through it now, half-aware, clacking
These heavy miles home. The gulls caw
And clang in my mind. We sing our ancestors,
The clay under our rocking feet. The birth
Of coal, he tells me, is death,

A film of soot that cracks open my eyes.

The Migrants

In rusty pickups
they come into the dawn-lit fields.
We see the dust rise
barely on motionless air.
When the too-slow trucks fall silent,
the migrants are out suckering tobacco.
Others chop stubborn grass,
learn the warmth of sun.
Everyone listens to chattering birds
who dive from oak to oak.
Sometimes the migrants are stunned
as though they have never heard such secrets.
Mist settles and glitters.
Soon, shadows will lighten.
Like the sky, the oak, pine,
and red maple slowly wake.

YUSEF KOMUNYAKAA

The Whistle

1

The seven o'clock whistle
Made the morning air fulvous
With metallic syncopation,
A key to a door in the sky—opening
& closing flesh. The melody
Men & women built lives around,
Sonorous as the queen bee's fat
Hum drawing workers from flowers,
Back to the colonized heart.
A titanous puff of steam rose
From the dragon trapped below
Iron, bricks, & wood.
The whole machine
Shuddered: blue jays & redbirds
Wove light through leaves
& something dead under the foundation
Brought worms to life.
Men capped their thermoses,
Switched off Loretta Lynn,
& slid from trucks & cars.
The rip saws throttled
& swung out over logs
On conveyor belts.
Daddy lifted the tongs
To his right shoulder . . . a winch
Uncoiled the steel cable
From its oily scrotum;
He waved to the winchman
& iron teeth bit into pine.

Yellow forklifts darted
With lumber to boxcars
Marked for distant cities.
At noon, Daddy would walk
Across the field of goldenrod
& mustard weed, the pollen
Bright & sullen on his overalls.
He'd eat on our screened-in
Back porch—red beans & rice
With ham hocks & cornbread.
Lemonade & peach Jello.

The one o'clock bleat
Burned sweat & salt into afternoon
& the wheels within wheels
Unlocked again, pulling rough boards
Into the plane's pneumatic grip.
Wild geese moved like a wedge
Between sky & sagebrush,
As Daddy pulled the cable
To the edge of the millpond
& sleepwalked cypress logs.
The day turned on its axle
& pyramids of russet sawdust
Formed under corrugated
Blowpipes fifty feet high.
The five o'clock whistle
Bellowed like a bull, controlling
Clocks on kitchen walls;
Women dabbed loud perfume
Behind their ears & set tables
Covered with flowered oilcloth.

* * *

2

When my father was kicked by the foreman,
He booted him back,
& his dreams slouched into an aftershock
Of dark women whispering
To each other. Like petals of a black rose
In one of Busby Berkeley's
Oscillating dances in a broken room. Shadows,
Runagates & Marys.
The steel-gray evening was a canvas
Zigzagged with questions
Curling up from smokestacks, as dusky birds
Brushed blues into a montage
Traced back to *L'Amistad* & the psychosis
Behind *Birth of a Nation.*
With eyes against glass & ears to diaphanous doors,
I heard a cornered prayer.
Car lights rubbed against our windows,
Ravenous as snow wolves.
A brick fell into the living room like a black body,
& a riot of drunk curses
Left the gladioli and zinnias
Maimed. Double dares
Took root in night soil.
The whistle boiled
Gutbucket underneath silence
& burned with wrath.
But by then Daddy was with Uncle James
Outside The Crossroad,
Their calloused fingers caressing the .38
On the seat of the pickup;
Maybe it was the pine-scented moonglow
That made him look so young
& faceless, wearing his mother's powder blue
Sunday dress & veiled hat.

Red Blessings

for Edna B., my mother

1
Straw hat on
Old clothes on
Moma's down
In the tomato field
Sitting on back the tiller
Dropping seeds in the earth.
Moma's down in the field
On back the tiller.
Her apron's full of seeds
Her mouth full of smiles.

2
Cracked hands.
Moma's cracked hands peel
Buckets and buckets of tomatoes
For 50 cents a bucket
Until she can stand and peel no more.
Moma peels buckets and buckets of tomatoes
And she stands in clear plastic boots
On wet, juiced concrete floors.
She breathes a steamy funk and dreams of oceans
Without middle passages.
Moma peels buckets of tomatoes.
All I can do at dusk is pump water
Over her vinyl apron and rubber gloves
Watch yellow-green seeds swirl away

•   •   •

3

Moma sits cross-legged at a gray picnic table
Eating Sunday ham with mustard (only, thank-you) on Wonder bread.
She chitchats, "Girl, stop!"
With her cannery mates
Balancing on upturned baskets.
They chew their food
Slow
Swat at musty migrant men telling lies and green flies,
Their black-mesh hair nets
Attached to white paper visors imprinted
With "Choptank Canning Co."
Who pays them Fridays in cash.
"Child, see you afta I get my hair done."

4

I scrub Moma's back
Rub white alcohol
On her skin
To cool her mind.
She sleeps.

5

White paint flecks brown, bowed marsh grass
Lining windswept cannery with sagging roof
Roost of crows and bats.
I swim through cobwebs
Stand where once ivory,
High-yellow, redbone, brown-sugar and blue-black
Women
Sorted, cored, peeled and cooked red blessings
Until they could find something better.
"Till Lawd, somethin' better."

. . .

6
Moma's gray.
Tired.
Can't wear coral lipstick.
Can't snap her fingers.
Can't get down like she used to.
She's buried
her smiles
three men
beneath sinking sands
The Conductor and Douglass
Eluded.

At the Owl Club, North Gulfport, Mississippi, 1950

Nothing idle here—the men
so casual, each lean, each
tilted head and raised glass
a moment's stay from work.

Son Dixon's center of it all,
shouldering the cash register.
This is where his work is:
the New Orleans tailored suits,

shining keys, polished wood
and mirrors of the bar.
A white Cadillac out front.
Money in his pocket, a good cigar.

The men gather here after work.
a colored man's club. Supper
served in the back—gumbo, red beans,
talk of the Negro Leagues.

They repeat in leisure
what they've done all day—
stand around the docks, waiting
for a call, for anything to happen,

• • •

a chance to heave crates of bananas
and spiders. A risky job, its only
guarantee the consolation check
for a dead man's family.

Their lace-up boots say *shipyard.*
Dirt-caked trousers, *yard work.*
Regal Quarts in hand—
It's payday man.

Pea Song

black eyed peas
will make a sista mean

fight ya for 'em
till the grass ain't green

knew a girl named Black-Eyed Sue
she kept the peas in a high-laced shoe

she said

I can't start my new year right
unless my peas is outta sight

Nana kept 'em in a pocketbook
same as Tab and dear Aunt Sook

Mama kept 'em in her dresser drawer
drawls scented with the onion core

turkey butt pepper Lawry's
make ya shit out cowries

c'mon

black eyed peas
will make a sista mean

fight ya for 'em
till the grass ain't green

CARRIE ALLEN McCRAY

Intermittent Requiems for Bud

tribute to Bud Powell, the great jazz pianist

I listen to "Cherokee" and try
to keep up with the beat.
You run over the keys like
Owens on the turf, powerful,
bursting into the finish line,
like that last moment of love.
The great Miles said he learned
"cool" from you, called you genius.
What stirred you, what demons
possessed you?
At ease, only at the piano,
tranquil there,
then blue deep into a funk,
sitting motionless now on the
piano stool,
distance in your sweet smile.
Your lady says "hello,"
you are not there.
She says "hello" again,
waves her hand across your
glazed eyes.
"Gone Again," she smiles, "but
he'll come back.
When he does, I'll ask him
to play 'Yesterdays.' "

Like the sun after a storm,
her words penetrate your haze,
then you come back to us
and play her request.

Witness

After the concert by Marian Anderson sponsored by the Phillis Wheatley Literary Club, Charleston, 1926

We rode your voice through Handel and Debussy,
our backs straight.

The sun-swallowing bloom of your soprano,
measured and wild.

Your hand on the piano,
you in its curve.

Glossolalia in our throats
as the spirituals washed down.

Sometimes I feel like a motherless child

Dere's no hidin' place down dere

Monday night became Sunday morning
and you had a choir, Marian.

You had a brand new choir.

The Spice of Life

cayenne in our blood
we dance, eat, laugh, cry & love
with peppered passion

The Quilter

for L. Teresa Church

        She stitches in a little piece of each
new place she goes, the blocks a road map she'll
        key for you on cue, a kind of cloth speech
inscribed in fabric culled from every real

        town she's seen (the ones that boast at least a Wal-
Mart selling bright remnants). Strip-mall strips: one
        swatch marks the spot. And she stitches in small
squares of everyone she loves: patterns done

        just like her grandma taught her, colors planned
yet random—squash-yellow, tomato-red,
        beet-purple, solids, prints—a plot of land
where she plants scraps of old dresses, shirts. Bred

        and called, she pieces scattered kin and foot-
steps together: her strong thread, a long root.

Sound and Semblance

—"mu" twenty-sixth part—

    A sand-anointed wind spoke of
survival, wood scratched raw,
   scoured bough. And of low sky
     poked at by branches,   blown
rush,   thrown voice,   legbone
                          flute . . .
    Wind we all filled up with caught
   in the tree we lay underneath . . .
Tree filled up with wind and more
                      wind,
   more than could be said of it said . . .
   So-called ascendancy of shadow,
   branch, would-be roost, now not
     only a tree, more than a tree . . .

It was the bending of boughs we'd
    read about, Ibn 'Arabi's reft
ipseity, soon-come condolence,
                  thetic
    sough. We saved our breath, barely
                   moved,
    said nothing, soon-come suzerainty
volubly afoot,   braided what we'd
   read and what we heard and what
    stayed sayless,   giggly wind,
                  wood,

riffling wuh . . .   A Moroccan
   reed-flute's desert wheeze took
our breath,   floor we felt we
      stood on, caustic earth we rode
across . . . It was Egypt or Tennessee
                                          we
      were in. No one, eyes exed out,
   could say which. Fleet, millenarian
   we it now was whose arrival the wind
                                          an-

nounced

   —————

   Night found us the far side of
Steal-Away Ridge, eyes crossed
   out, X's what were left, nameless
      what we saw we not-saw. We ducked
   and ran, rained on by tree-sap,
                                          dreaming,
chattered at by wind and leaf-stir,
      more than we'd have dreamt or
   thought. We lay on our backs looking
   up at the limbs of the tree we lay
      underneath, leaves our pneumatic
                                          book,
   We lay on our backs' unceased reprise.

North of us was all an emolument,
   more than we'd have otherwise run.
We worked at crevices, cracks,
   convinced we'd pry love loose,
                          wrote
our names out seven times in dove's
                        blood,
    kings and queens, crowned ourselves
  in sound. Duke was there,   Pres, Lady,
   Count,   Pharaoh came later. The
Soon-Come Congress we'd heard so much
   about, soon come even sooner south . . .
                        So

    there was a new mood suddenly, blue
                  but uptempo,
parsed, bitten into,   all of us got our
share . . . Pecks what had been kisses, beaks
  what once were lips, other than we
were as we lay under tree limbs, red-beaked
                  birds
   known as muni what we were, heads crowned
                    in

  sound only in
 sound

Cookout

Blackish
grey
gnarled
like
ancient
rough
cragging
stones
oysters
poured
hot
rustled
from
the
big
boiling
pot
out
onto
ripened
board
table
each
by
each
knife
tip
pried
gently
easing

open
secret
seasoned
juiciness
Geechee
blessed

Watermelon Repast

Landscape verdant to brush
Driving up Highway 85, moving for the third time,
north-south, south-north, south-west
Toes drying lilac fantasy in the dashboard sun

Battery light pulses, car sputters, slows, stops
"A Good Man Is Hard to Find" reminds me
Not to flag down the wrong car
I leave in search of a curtain

End up squatting in a melon patch
Watering the dry red earth as wasps float
From melon to melon, suckle, roll off
Collide like winos, unable to stop sipping

I see them swollen with sun and can't resist
Perfect, jade-striped skin, oblong
Humming of barbecues and baptisms
Mosquitoes and fingers sticky with pink

I carry it back to the car, low against my womb
Together we split it on the hood
At this unmarked rest stop
Two miles south of Sweetwater

The melon keeps its promise
As the tow truck arrives

JOANNE GABBIN

Pot Meals

in memory of Jessie Smallwood Veal

Pot meals hold so many possibilities.
Not like meat, potatoes, beets
Discriminately sectioned on the plate,
No red touching brown, or brown
Intruding its rudeness on white fluff.
In Mama's kitchen neck bones add
Their gray-brown juices to string beans and potatoes
Whistling and sputtering in the family pot.

No food is measured out in small portions
Or hidden New York style until company leaves.
When Cousin James comes by to gossip,
His head ticking slightly as he keeps company with words,
Mama just adds a little water to the beans
And makes an extra pan of biscuits.
Her mother told her how to stretch a pot.
"Add what you have," she said. "Love multiplies."

Mama knows how to make food multiply;
Like the sacred meal it swells to feed the multitude.
Comfort food for Aunt Mae
Who has moon shoulders today.
After dinner she lays her head
On the cool marble-top table;
Little Sis gets the black small-tooth comb
And begins to scratch her troubles out.

. . .

Now when I want to remember Mama,
To bring back the woman
Whose only vanity was her reputation
As a scrupulously clean cook,
In whose kitchen nothing was wasted
And no one turned away,
I get out the family pot, add love
And cook up some possibilities.

i know the grandmother one had hands

i know the grandmother one had hands
but they were always in bowls
folding, pinching, rolling the dough
making the bread
i know the grandmother one had hands
but they were always under water
sifting rice
blueing clothes
starching lives
i know the grandmother one had hands
but they were always in the earth
planting seeds
removing weeds
growing knives
burying sons
i know the grandmother one had hands
but they were always under
the cloth
pushing it along
helping it birth into
skirt
dress
curtains to lock out
night
i know the grandmother one had hands
but they were always inside
the hair
parting
plaiting
twisting it into rainbows

i know the grandmother one had hands
but they were always inside
pockets
holding the knots
counting the twisted veins
holding onto herself
lest her hands disappear
into sky
i know the grandmother one had hands
but they were always inside the clouds
poking holes for the
rain to fall.

Smoke

Your father turns the rib eye on the grill. In a few days he'll leave home
for field duty. You watch him get lost in the puff of new smoke.
It is like flipping a record over after the last song:

He slips his fingers on the vinyl, scratched and worn,
skating the dark circle. He does not know
his wife will thin the night and the linoleum
in a slow dance made for two.

In a weekend ritual, he bends over those old album covers:
Cash, Waylon, Campbell, their liquor red-eye and his.
Their superstar cowboy brims, your daddy's boonie hat,
their throats cut with gold and diamonds,
around your father's neck a noose dragging a dog tag.

" . . . *cow-boy, dun-dun*", your father sings,
the chorus of fallen leaves crackling in the drainage ditch.
You wave away smoke to get a good look at him.
He smiles, and you worry when he does it with all his teeth exposed.
It's the kind of grin reserved for beer and barbecue and Sundays.

You try to sing along too to *something rhinestone*
but you get the words wrong. Your papi lights up,
a tobacco puff blows your way, fragrant like cinnamon.
He does not look at you; instead, he looks around
at everything he'll never own, though he signed for it.

• • •

Daughters and scraps of credit and memory. Children,
cornhusks blocking out his sky. Five mouths and a broken dial
on the pawnshop Sanyo. All he gets now is snow
in someone's coal miner daughter.

Give him room, a cloud of smoke whispers, tells you to go away,
let your Papi do his thing. The smoke collars him, turns his hair white.
There's a devil in the next track. You know what comes next.
He's listening for clues, even in the scratches.

He is far gone, already turned to a secret B side, tuned to a twang
you cannot hear, blue forest floors in his eyes,
all the backcountry of his mind. The ditches he'll dig,
holes he'll slip into. You'll always wonder

if all the voices that called were in his mother's tongue
or if they carried all the dusts of Clarksville.

Middle Ear

Say that moment crossing over isn't heard
Say the hammer-anvil-stirrup don't unfurl
Say the balance was upset

Say this balance was upset
Say the outside world doesn't ring

Say the mind's ear listening to an odd man singing
Say the moment crossing over starting somewhere out and in
Say the balance was upset

Say this balance was upset, and the singing falls faint
Say you turn yourself away from crowds of sound

Say the awed man singing sings to you

Say you don't know him. You don't.

And the balance is upset

Say the inside singing and the outside ringing and
      the moment crossing over breathing in
Say the whisper of the man sieves through
Say the moment crossing over is a stranger wisp

And the balance is upset
And the balance is upset

• • •

Say the moment crossing over rights the left
Say the moment crossing over is the ringing ear writing
Say the moment crossing over ends hear

Don't Get Your Hot Hair Wet
or Your Good Shoes Dirty

How to Teach Them

1. Grooming
Maybe she saw God the Father lurking
behind each seven-year-old's face—
thirty pairs of eyes watching her, judging.

For twenty-odd years the same crop of bad
and good—their mamas, uncles, cousins.
So many ruined. Insolent. Unkempt.

Thirty offspring every year,
she never wanted to push one
out of herself. What world

could they have outside her own?
How to teach them that happiness
would come only from acceptance,

that beauty begins with cleanliness.
Her classroom was as orderly
as her childless home.

2. Beauty
TV pageants had shown us
how to line up, be sorted.

I pitied the boys who had to pick us.
They must've seen those contests too.

• • •

What we saw had everything to do
with love, the promise of it.

The screen was a greedy mirror
withholding the goods,

reflecting our hunger. Desire
and denial, at once, our ration.

At school, we learned those adult dramas,
learned that our bodies could betray us.

Our teacher urging each one,
the boys chose eagerly,

shunning the darker girls, their moving
lips, their accusing eyes.

3. Economics
When Mrs. Harris slapped my brother
his nose bled—an instant protest.
It kept up for hours—at school, on the bus,
at home. Neither the silver key hung
down his back on a string nor the wad
of brown paper under his lip could quell it.
We didn't consider charges, a lawsuit,
but accepted the principal's astute
offer: a year of free lunch.

4. Citizenship
One white teacher in a black school,
young and pretty, her place assured.

We learned about belonging
from a civics assignment:

• • •

Find out the origins
of our family names.

My father's answer made perfect
sense to me, though it angered her:

They came from the slave master—
that's how our people got them.

Yours? From a white man called Strange.

Immolatus

She had her feet in the trough,
Nosing into the golden corn,
When daddy did a half spin
& brought down the sledgehammer.
She sank to the mud.
An oak branch bowed
As they tightened the rope
To a creaky song of pulley wheels.
A few leaves left
For the wind to whip down,
They splashed hot water
& shaved her with blades
That weighed less each year.
Snow geese honked overhead
& Sirius balanced on a knifetip.
Wintertime bit into the ropy guts
Falling into a number-3 tub
That emptied out in a gray gush
Like the end of a ditch
Choked with slime & roses.
Something love couldn't make
Walk again. I had a boy's job
Lugging water from the pump
& filling the iron washpot.
I threw pine knots on the blaze.
Soon her naked whiteness
Was a silence to split
Between
helpers & owner.
Liver, heart, & head

Flung to a foot tub.
They smiled as she passed
Through their hands. Next day
I tracked blood in a circle
Across dead grass, while fat
Boiled down to lye soap.

Nikki-Rosa

childhood memories are always a drag
if you're Black
you always remember things like living in Woodlawn
with no inside toilet
and if you become famous or something
they never talk about how happy you were to have
your mother
all to yourself and
how good the water felt when you got your bath
from one of those
big tubs that folk in Chicago barbecue in
and somehow when you talk about home
it never gets across how much you
understood their feelings
as the whole family attended meetings about Hollydale
and even though you remember
your biographers never understand
your father's pain as he sells his stock
and another dream goes
And though you're poor it isn't poverty that
concerns you
and though they fought a lot
it isn't your father's drinking that makes any difference
but only that everybody is together and you
and your sister have happy birthdays and very good
Christmases
and I really hope no white person ever has cause
to write about me
because they never understand
Black love is Black wealth and they'll

probably talk about my hard childhood
and never understand that
all the while I was quite happy

Lessons in Trailer Living

My grandmother used to catch mice.
The trailer skittered under the muse of their visitations.

We would discover them in the morning, gutted like red snapper
on the linoleum, the chase still on their small faces.

Lesson one: Death is the machination of old women,
hell-bent on keeping a clean house.

Lesson two: Death happens at night, a force maneuvering
through the dark in wild thumping motions.

Lesson three: A mouse was dead
and we could not outwardly grieve for him,

though he reminded us of clocks striking one
and murderous farmers' wives.

Poor little Daleville Trailer Park mouse
mistaking our home for refuge,

finding a place where bread and children are tucked away,
secret as the poison in arsenic.

Hair Raising

blue magic scalp, hair
burning in the kitchen, Grandma
resting in my nose

1957

my father
was in chicago

a city
without telephones
envelopes

post or
western union offices

i did not know that
in 1957

only the way to
tom's

where moon pies

were the perfect
substitution

when georgia haze

obscured the one
night rider
we did not
fear

• • •

someone with a rope-thick
accent
called me boy

did he
mean to get
my attention?

i left my moon pies on the counter

i was three.

Manhood

1.
Streetlights ghost
white, chalk-in silhouette of concern,
eyes black with dread, knees shake inside
the bones. Soon there will be yellow
CRIME SCENE tape, camera flashes
to match the spotlights, detective eyes
of interest; but for now, a worried-skinned
woman, the man's mother, crouches
as if she could feed life back into his,
as if he is still a growing boy in need
of her. But he isn't. He doesn't.
He lies there stomach and palms down,
hands cupping concrete
the way he'd cup his baby boys' cheeks,
as if he could butterfly swim his way out
of the bullet that pierced his back
activating a different kind of volcano,
one that swallows his classic button-down shirt,
that smolders his breathing, blown-away
ash, but doesn't burn.
He was twenty-six, leaves two sons and his mother,
who at least knows her baby will finally
sleep with both eyes closed.

•   •   •

2.

Sleep with both eyes closed
when you're dead, the daddy always told
his sons. They have his cheeks, his eyes,
only theirs still glimmer hope and
pray for every step they take.
Eyes, one open, are both absent
of sleep, absent of dreams—
grown before their age,
dead before their time.
A Black man never cries, the daddy
also told his sons and they didn't. Nothing
on them did. They just sat, their little denim-
clothed bottoms in the same classic button-up.
Daddy dressed them to match him. On
the hood of his car, the one they knew:
never get out of and always put on
the seatbelt, the one that played Otis Redding
because sittin' on the dock of a bay
was a nice thought far away from the cold
streets and fast money, and
whistling always sounded like their age.
Both were safe behind those tinted windows.
Remember to always see out
but never let anyone see in,
the daddy said, driving through peekaboo
streetlights, letting his sons do the math.

what she will remember

she is afraid to step into the rows
of cotton   afraid time will stop/rewind
itself back into past recollections
where she is eight   ash black and shielded

from her father's neck still handling scars
of coarse rope and night-rider prayers
for willow trees weeping   she is afraid
her mother will shoot and miss

her next birthday   break the promise
always to watch over the rough-skin girl
she is afraid the wind will turn her back
give out and betray their friendship for the first time

there are no-good white men waiting
with coke bottle penises between the stalks
they remain empty and cold on the river's bed
they have been asleep she is afraid to tell me

for quite some time   she has been afraid
to teach me how to walk the rows step feet
first onto red dust and move past each stalk
slowly becoming something we never forget.

Splinter of the Path

We drop hips and spin.
Dervishes locked in
a collective vision quest.

High-Top *All-Stars*
pound staccato
on dust-layered clay.

Sun drenched, mad.
We forge rivers
of scarred flesh,
challenging the myths
of the playground.

Bodies twist skyward,
searching for a finger roll
sweet as Ice-Man Gervin's.
A jumper that can add
two more *O*s to smooth.

Orphaned beyond
ancestry, we yearn
for any rite of passage:
Drum of feet.
Dance of muscle.

• • •

By chance, we
found this capoeira
of ball and hoop
and bled it black.
Now

Our dance is
Spin
for dark flesh mounds
under the sway of hips.

Our chant is
Jump
for mahogany moons
swelled behind navels.

Our drum is
Stomp
for brown suckling breasts
between lips and fingers.

Our song is
Scream
for the earth where we learn
the worship of all things round.

Fusion

       As a girl, I made lists.
A student of high-fashion
    and only ifs—
how to mimic pouty lips and
       a tousled fresh-from-bed head
guaranteed to put you back in with a man
    according to *Cosmo* mavens.

       My mom slipped *Ebony*
under my bedroom door, where I mixed
    hot wax tricks for instant bare limbs.
    I wanted to be thin and beyond

       recognition. To blend in
    with appleblushed cheeks and
hair twirling fingertips. The white girls
    got the Science and Phys. Ed. teachers' looks,
"Isn't she something."

       I wanted to cry
my way out of speeding tickets and into
    boys' arms. Why wouldn't mom make
potatoes and sloppy joes instead of catfish
and chitlins?

    . . .

I resolved to be like them.
                    Number one: shave
          armpits; number two: relax
hair straight, curl and hitch
          the cascades in place with Still Life spray.
Mom said it's a sin
to get rid of what God gives.

You're gorgeous!

    The shocker was turning hip,
the teenage goal—to be un-
          usual—the girls called me unique.
I was an exotic garden
          to walk through. I was so not
like the other girls they knew. It was a complimentary
ticket to get close; then
I received invites for putt-putt and sleepovers.
We were the only black family
          on the block. When we moved in,
              the neighbors brought Bundt cakes
          and removed their shoes before entering.
              We were immigrants
          to neighborhood associations
and cul-de-sacs. Yes, we'd have to have them

over for dinner; then mom shut the door
     before asking me if they'd like her
special: oxtail stew over grits.
                    Only if, only if—
my mantra for a curse and a wish.

On the first drive-by

my family of five packs "the brown tank,"
four-door fortress—a Ford not made any more.
On a Sunday cruise, a car passes, wide tires,
white hide, like the General Lee, bleached.
Every seat filled: a wizard at the wheel,
a shotgun lookout & two backseat drivers
ready to spit & roll, throw sharp tongues
from soiled mouths to scream

        niggers.

        Mother & Father
can't bring themselves to speak,
brother & sister my bone-flesh
bookends. Our car keeps rolling,
no hum, like the engine is scared
to burn.
        There will be reruns,
without Uncle Jesse,
Bo & Luke,
or a Waylon Jennings sound track.
        These strangers won't visit
via TV. This word will rage
until the last ear is gouged.

Mama Gertie Bell Speaks to Her Granddaughter

Cher,
I could snap a chicken's neck
with just three whips of my arm,
slash a cottonmouth in half
with one swoop of a shovel.
I bared down and spilt
Love out of my womb,
and raised your daddy
while I raised myself.
I looked at myself in the mirror
when all my children was gone.
I wore high heels till the day I died.

That long metallic bayou runs
silver through your veins.
You are the tall sugarcane in the fields
slow-dragging in the September breeze,
holding tight your roots.
A brown pecan
plump with sweet meat
protected by a stubborn shell.
And you are the magnolia
thick, sturdy petals bursting open
trying to reach the sun,
spilling the sweet smell of Now
into summer heat.

Chil',
You ain't never got to beg nobody to love you.

My Best Day

Summer
we walk the concrete
Me, Sukie, and Laconya
with dusty feet
midriff tops
cutoff shorts

Past knee-high grass
purple and fuchsia wildflowers
june bugs
Liberate blackberries from the vine
—"Don't worry 'bout no snakes."

Join a gathering of elders
eighteen to twenty-five
A lean ebony sapling
grins white and gold
He shares his forty with us
Another, watermelon

The sun tucks itself in
In youthful innocence
we await tomorrow

Do it all over again

Nicknames

for Darrell Haley

> We must learn to wear our names
> within all the noise and confusion
> of the environment in which we find ourselves;
> make them the center of all our associations
> with the world, with man and with nature.
> We must charge them with all our emotions,
> our hopes, hates, loves, aspirations.
> They must become our masks and our shields
> and the containers of all those values
> and traditions which we learn and/or imagine
> as being the meaning of our familial past.
> — Ralph Ellison

We could signify.
Any twin was Twin.
The shape of Moe's head
made him Dick,
slang for the male organ.
Darryl was Tee Tee,
the asthmatic noise
he made whenever
he ran. Anybody
with a limp, Crip.

. . .

Girls had it worse.
Feel sorry for Tawana,
so short so brown
she was called Roach.
Also Ernestine, better known
as Teeny Weeny
because she was
flat-chested and had
a small behind
like a boy's.

Whatever.
My man Meat
wanted to box. Boo coach.
Poobie design clothes.
What stopped them?
Andre's dark side,
Drako, got him locked-up.
Black Eddie was shot
in the back by a cop
during a hold-up.

Go Ju go Ju go.
Lightskinned Rainbow
eclipsed Tick Tock,
his chocolate walk-partner.
Incestuous Pinky and Tan.
Both Frogs. Squirrel. Crazy ass Sponge.
Bama Duke's lopsided,
sticky daughter, Peaches.
Our b-shaped barber,
Blinky. We miss you

. . .

Missy, rest in peace.
John Rocks-on-Rocks.
The Young Dillingers.
Freckles versus Baby Tim.
Cabalou stuttering,
i-m-m-mi-t-ta-ting Johnny Lips.
Hillbilly, Lefty, Itchy and Skip.
Dootie Bug's first
baby's mama, leaving.
Tootie had Fin.

Lucky lucky me: Sayers
because I was fast
and Sticks because I was skinny.
Spanish Doug. Erno. Shoe and Ding.
The Immaculate Conception
and Gibson Plaza Apartments
double-baptizing poverty.
Oldhead Jimbo spoiling
healthy baby girls
Stuff or Boo.

Born busy and still busy,
our restless senses typecast
Jerry Green as Dirty Jerry,
Fat Dave as himself
and all four Lightfoots as Light.
Alcohol took Redbone
from Redds & The Boys.
Reader, you figure
Kerry's mama's
dozen for Mess.

. . .

Imagine, then, the scars
spared flawed iris Dot-Eye
and Heavy-One's inability to dodge
the percussive dice roll
of random gunfire.
Cherry trees that blossom,
blister and bleed.
God's called upon
home-ruled hands,
pocketing Footz.

Journeyman

Fourteen and the color of lemons,
He breathes hay and hickory,

Rolls cigarettes, practices slow inhales
Behind the barn. Whisper of a boy in

Homemade shoes, humming himself a life.
When the time comes, he wraps biscuits

And fried chicken in a blue kerchief.
Finds the sweet tobacco and papers

His brother hides under the mattress.
He wants new shoes, a pretty big-legged

Girl to moan him a lowdown juke.
He dreams of solitary blues on boxcars

From Tuscaloosa to Gulfport, a journeyman's
Seduction to mannish ways. Tonight, he stands

Under a canopy of pecan trees waiting for a rush
Of diesel wind and the timbre of Norfolk rail.

Buckwheat's Lament

My family tells me this white gang I run with will
Grow up, and leave me behind. Our bones
Will change, and so will their affection. I will
Be a childlike man who lives in a shack. Just
Wait, they promise, my hair will become
Hoo-doo. The white girls will deny how we rassled,
What we saw. They laugh

Wait 'til you're *grown*. And I hear this sad place
At the middle of that word where they live,
Where they wait for my skin to go sour.

bull

the whoppers my father could tell—

that he walked to school and back /
without shoes / in ninety-eight-degree sun /
on blazing rocks and an empty stomach /
every day / until he was seventeen;

of the time when he and sugarpig beat down all the brutes
who lived up on the hook—*cause you know them boys would*
cut your throat and steal the heart right outta your chest and
that's why most of them are in jail or dead today—yeah,
he and sugarpig sent them home scared and crying;

or the time he had to fight the devil for his guitar. how the horny red little
    urchin
with a bow-and-arrow tail and swamp-lizard skin marched with his
    pitchfork right into
my grandmomma's front door (she and granddaddy at church, of course)
    and snatched
daddy's Fender acoustic by the strings, in the middle of "jesus keep me near
    the cross." daddy poured a gallon of lipton sun tea on that joker's head and
    watched him holler all the way back to hell.

. . .

we knew all the yak by heart,
watched daddy scratch his head
and shuck his shoes to the side
to gnash into the next story.

our charge every time
to listen, on the brink of our seats,
teary ducts, eyes red.

How to Make It

If you turn out the bathroom lights
and whisper three times
Mary Weatherbee, I killed your husband
Mary Weatherbee, I killed your husband
Mary Weatherbee, I killed your husband
the old hag will reach out of the mirror
and scratch your face
so never whisper
those words in a dark bathroom
or anywhere else.

Count the cars in a funeral procession
and your fingers will walk off
in the middle of the night.
If you and another person
say the same thing
at the same time
knock wood first
so you are the sound
not the echo.

.   .   .

See a dead animal
lying in the road
Spit
to get the bad taste
out of your mouth.
Be the first
to wish on the first star
and your wish will come true.

Sidewalk cracks
are your mother's back
fine fissures in a fragile universe.

An empty wagon
keeps a lot of noise
so be quiet
and you will be full.
When you play jacks
the scatter has to be larger
than the largest hand
in the game or it's
Scatter's over.

Learn to conjugate
"to be" and "to have"
and you will.

Do not ask
do not whisper
do not wonder
if someone three streets over
or three time zones over
whispered before you
I wish I may, I wish I might.

. . .

You are too small
to predict the future
so if your mother is late getting home
protect her—
imagine the unspeakable
and it will not speak—

she will return to you precious
and mostly whole.

Do not ask
How do you count first,
the starting point of a sphere.
Know you must be the first and be the first
whispering your rosary dreams
into the squeezed night
of shut eyelids.
I wish I may, I wish I might.

And if you call for
Mary Weatherbee
if you count the funeral cars
if you forget the number of cracks
if you fall asleep
waiting on your mother
and wake too late
if they let you be first,
you can still
sit up and spit, child,
spit.
Look at the jack shining
across the dirt of heaven
and demand to see
the hand of God.

key west

you could have
buried emmett till
beneath that maze
of granules
at the bottom
of the dixie cup
i was handed
(minus lemon)
through the
jim crow window
of peaches cafe
key west florida
may 1960

i swore i saw a blonde
smile
through the
fancy restaurant window

but mother said
she was picking
stone crab
from beneath her
teeth

• • •

and to turn
my eyes
toward heaven

where it seemed
to me
even the
sky and clouds

sat

apart.

COLLEEN J. McELROY

Eads Bridge Boogie Across the Mississippi

The way Mama tells it I didn't have the good sense
God gave a chinch much less know to stay away from fast
tail gals who danced across that river into evil Illinois.
But I was sixteen—you know the age—dreaming
about draping myself across some smoky piano, stocking
seams bone straight and skirt hiked thigh high
like Tina Turner on those nights when she was still
strutting low down in kitchen table clubs. I was jail
bait—a gun moll in my dreams—flying high inside
husky voice blues beside some boy with a come-on look till
the sun came up and I went racing racing home before
that dishwater light caught me on the wrong side
of the Mississippi—the bridge railings slicing shadows
across the water whuckity-whuck like Chuck Berry's guitar.
And that sweet brown boy with the gimme-some eyes
trying to turn sober and both of us, like Mama said:
looking like hell sued for murder.

SHIRLETTE AMMONS

History Makes Concessions for White Boys

from all my white sins forgiven, they feed
— Philip Levine, "They Feed They Lion"

At the Food Lion,
This cute one hangs and guts
The pot-bellied pork;
I suppose his kisses salt and slime,
Which would have appeased the high school me,
Ham gelatin swathing my tongue
As I lip-synced good vibrations
Like mark wahlberg wasn't just
A white boy in dropped boxers
Protesting the mullet

I remember his face now,
He and his girlfriend mashed like Juicy Fruit
In that big-ass, dixie-flagged, Ford F-150,
Me, a member of the yellow school-bus clique,
Sitting, suffocating, three deep in a pleathered seat;
Mexican, black, po white trash, cousins of cousins
Muddled like the fuzz between pecan trees
And AM radio stations;
Her hands, gold nugget promise rings,
Engaged his stringy hair;
As his dual mufflers fumed down Highway 403,
Racial divide scoured the windshields
Of our wheeled, county property

. . .

He steps outside between slaughterings
To smoke a red-boxed Marlboro.
I notice his bangs have grown out;
He stares as if my locks carry remnants
Of barrettes and blurred bus numbers;
We nod and smile, an understood country greeting;
I figure he and his girlfriend still coast cramped,
The same way public transportation taught us
To squeeze tight in our assigned seats
In case the white boy's pickup broke down

Why else would we make room for a passenger
Who never needed a ride?

Black Hymnal

for Addie Mae Collins,
after Alabama,
September 15, 1963

If Addie Mae Collins's spindly legs
had not been licked and swallowed
by flame and smoke, flesh splattered,
frail ashes amid funeral fans
and white tithe envelopes charred
to dusty debris

—Come Sunday—
would her feet follow the familiar
march to Zion, ample ankles springing
while she stepped, this Easter morning,
palms turned upwards, cupping the black
hymnal close, cupping the white
cross engraved above her heart?

—Come some Sunday—
how would the years age her, carved
crow's-feet edging her eyes, kettle
colored lashes thickly curling as her skin
must have when the fire of white heat
burned white crosses on black lawns,
singeing grass to ash?

. . .

—Come sweet Sunday—
would she pull open the door
to the Sixteenth Street Baptist
Church, step onto a burnished
ruby runner bleeding
up to the birch
choir pew?

—Come this Sunday—
Would she waltz down the warm rose aisle,
melodies rolling through a holy mouth agape
for an *agape* love greater than the fire burning
through the bush, the fire burning the church,
singing: *Come Sunday . . . Oh Come Sunday . . .*
that's the day . . .

The Dry Spell

Waking early
with the warming house
my grandmother knew what to do
taking care not to wake
Da Da   she cooked up a storm
in darkness   adding silent spices
and hot sauce

to stay cool. She ate later, alone
after the children had been gathered
and made to eat
her red eggs. Da Da rose
late, long after
the roosters had crowed
his name, clearing
an ashy throat
pulling on long
wooly underwear
to make him sweat

. . .

even more. *The fields have gone*
long enough without water
he liked to say, *so can I*
and when he returned
pounds heavier
from those thirsty fields
he was even cooler
losing each soaked
woolen skin
to the floor, dropping
naked rain in his
wife's earthen arms.

Spectaculations

Sometimes a child can save your life:
burn your throat on fermented lullabies
instead of Jim Beam, save your liver
from happening to cirrhosis and his friends,
make you playground and run like a cholera
victim to pick up antsy soccer kids. A child
gives you another day and the best thing
for you is another day.
                                Sometimes a son will carry
his father from nightclub to the car, to his house,
place him softly into his bed, clean up vomit on
his shirt, get prepared for night-shift factory gig
and break his wife off some syllabic comfort,
before crying on his breaks with worry and
laughing at others' jokes, still with worry,
and when he comes out of the night, back
into the daylight, beyond drawn curtains,
his smile will be a big big brilliance.

. . .

A daughter sometimes will sit mother down
and not cry till the next to last thud bounces
boom in her heart. Daughters want Mamas
to understand women don't accept rings
to bob and weave. There are blue rifts
Mamas don't need to comprehend; just
catch it coming, hear hook, get lost, before
snags and "wish-I-hads." Let her Mama
see rainbows she gave her daughter, listen
how Baby-girl's sonatas catch, lodge
thick in her throat.
                    A parent, most times,
will save a child by sniffing itty-bitty infant
toes or by washing their dirty butts in kitchen
sink or by kissing child they created on those
hot hot nights, where parent bellies were once
full on red wine, and the parents had no prophylactic—
just straight sperm. But the wanting is an ache
and parents accept solidifying epistemology
of a period, and the waiting and wanting,
the wanting in waiting, the all-things-of-it—
paramount, lest this wanting never a be.

Ghazal for My Mother

You taught me to remember everything but the fill of my own urn: to forgive.
So how can I forget how you still writhed under him like a saint, longing to
burn: to forgive?

My breasts were mere rumors under my dress; he raised it to see if they were
true.
You pulled belief down like a star; wish on it or it will be his turn to forgive.

Upon interrogation the windows confessed, *we looked but we did not see.*
On your patchwork quilt there's a house of grief with the door sewn shut. I,
too, yearn to forgive.

I would have given glaciers to be beloved as he is beloved;
"You came here shivering and small; you will die that way if you won't learn
to forgive."

Your reproach was his sanctuary; he fled to the *yes* of my little body.
Permit me the dreams of an orphan before you sing me to sleep (spurn, to
forgive).

Our first name is Sarah; did you know, when did you know it meant
"princess" in Hebrew?
I inherit your kingdoms of regret, christen me: *my child, too stern to forgive.*

The Lord Looks Out for Babies and Fools;
The Anvil of Heaven Murmuring

Sunday

floral
ladies fanning
on the downbeat, bring Him
sopranos trained over
mops and
linens

How to Make Rain

Start with the sun
piled weeks deep on your back   after
you haven't heard rain for an entire
growing season   and making sure to face
due north   spit twice into the red clay
stomp your silent feet   *waiting rain*
rain to bring the washing in   rain
of reaping   rusty tubs of rain   wish
aloud   to be caught in the throat
of the dry well   head kissing your back
a bent spoon for groundwater   to be
sipped from   *slow courting rain   rain*
that falls forever   rain which keeps
folks inside and makes late afternoon
babies   begin to bury childhood clothes
wrap them around stones   and skulls of
doves   then mark each place well enough
to stand the coming storm   *rain of our*
fathers   shoeless rain   the devil is
beating his wife rain   rain learned
early   in the bones   plant these scare
crow people face down   wing wing
and bony anchor   then wait until they
grow roots and skeletons   *sudden soaking*
rain that draws out the nightcrawler
rain of forgetting   rain that asks for
more rain   rain that can't help but
answer   what you are looking for
must fall   what you are looking for is
deep among clouds   what you want to see

is a girl selling kisses beneath cotton
wood   is a boy drowning inside the earth

The Tire Plant Is Struck by Lightning

She watches her husband fill his pipe
at his bureau and tilt a match in. The glow
tells her where the door is. The next morning
black tar falls from the sky in plastic leaves

like frail hands that disintegrate as they descend.
Her daughter is already standing at the stove.
The girl is the sort you tell *Stir*
and the girl will stand with the spoon

until steam and core disappear into sauce.
Her husband left early for the office
when the soft dark did not fade but fell
in crumbled bits. She is surprised

something so dark and gentle could land so loudly,
like a hundred footfalls thudding around the house,
the dark muttering follows her.
A long cord of smoke rises from the plant,

like Moses' God is watching from up high
in the bright blue. As she sweeps the porch clean
the tar continues to fall, replacing
each dark leaf as she clears it away.

Baptism

ancestral pearls so deep, so blue
blue oozes from a teeming swamp.
a river rolls its ancient silt gulfward.
a muddy voice rises. 'come here pretty
baby, come sit down on my cypress knee.
run your willowy fingers thru the speckled moss
of my oaken heart. jordan river so chilly
and cold, religion so sweet.' mary mary
mother of sweet hallelujahs, make way
for this wild explosion of jubilant
white-robed sisters settled to their feast
of succulent crabs and bisque.
you miracle-motored scooters along
inaccessible ways, intrepid seekers of depths,
bring back that summer breeze that soulful
drummer breeze. stir this simmering black
pot to a cauldron of fructifying memory.
swirl this stagnant blood, this cold
streaming liquid pearl. trouble
this rooted tongue . . .

* * *

were you there when the preacher he dunked
sweet hannah deep down the western bank
and she rose white-robe-clinging wet
out of pearly blue blaze?—go down,
sweet hannah! run, river: trouble my song.
were you on the set when black king
of the blues-fiery throat traded in
his box for a travelin piano?—made
the levee his road, the sure way of
the river?—willow his tent, rock his
pillow, cold cold ground his bed?—
were you there? if you saw the sun
lay its thousand daily kisses the breadth
of that muddy bosom, felt the river bed
rock in the cradle of its mighty run
and the cypress swamp turn its oozing
blues to gold in the deep of midnight,
you were there. saw blue and coal
black king saw him sing. heard his
deep timbre entwine with another
sweet as rose water and old as wine.
black magnolia of the valley, queen
of the gold scissors. cleanest
belly button maker this side eden.
king singing from the midnight coal
black and blueness of his lonesome
road, his sad/happy song swaddling the wail
at the pearly root of this lifelicking tongue.

St. Philip Blues

It was Sunday
she had on Billie's dress
and wore Lena's look
some little girl grown up to be
big sportin' her stuff
in a garden in New Orleans
around the corner from Bayou St. John
with melody floatin' in the air
and Magnolia smellin' up the place

who would have thought
one and a half years ago
when she came ridin' in
on a note of Delta distinction
that she would go out so grand
a star at a filmmaker's house
singin' that old familiar tune
if it ain't broke, baby
then don't fix it
as the black dog barks
and the neighborhood children
on a wing and a prayer
shout as she opens the gate
to let in the artist from St. James
who painted the *tignon* queen

• • •

often my grandmother
told me stories like this
about women who came
floatin' down the Miss'sippi
with a gardenia in their hair
whistlin' they got rhythm
who could ask for anything mo'

oh, but *mais oui, chère*
the night was young
the June bugs were jumpin'
and Philli-man had the flash rollin'
technology in the dark, he said
that could capture any moment
so as not to miss
the rose petal attraction
in baby doll pink
on a sea of sky blue satin

don't get nuttin' on that dress
the crowd yelled
lift up that skirt, baby
so it won't trail the dust
turn to the downriver side
give us that best pose
show us what yo' mamma gave you
'cause it's Sunday, darlin'
and you got on that Billie dress
and wearin' that Lena look
some little girl grown up to be
big sportin' her stuff.

Quarter Moon Rise

soft moon shimmers out
of cloudy dress, stirred by night's
suggestive caress

Israelites

1

The house my grandmother built
was sacred. *Only the Lord,*
she professed, resided within its walls.
There, she marked her doors like the Jews in Egypt
etched *The blood of Jesus* on entryways,
red stains of pain—sacrificial blood—
her protection for firstborn son,
man of the house, her heir,
and controller of legacy she'd leave.
Decades she prayed against harm's approach,
shielded against Satan's wrath with air-cross
drawn through whispered psalms.
She sung sorrows, as David did,
to her Father. Warrior, she fought
battles beyond this physical realm.

2

Grandma, they're going to sell
the sanctuary you built, ark
for those torrential storms you
waded through. Those words will
vanish, I know. Greed's got an offering
so glorious—the lands of your Jerusalem
will be turned over soon. Let your tongues
stir up the angels you used to call upon.
Guard our souls. The place of peace
you promised is vanishing, and I fret—
for tomorrow, we may be a people
with no home.

Picnic

A lone woman stakes out a bench,
prepares her barbeque far from
splashes of insubordinate children.
Though the day is warm for autumn,
she wears a black velour jogging suit
as if to shield her smooth, unwrinkled
jet skin from the last rays of sun.

She smiles as I pass, full of my own purpose.
I am afraid she will ask me to join her.
Her hands betray a need for company
as she unscrews the caps of soda,
unfolds a plastic, checkered tablecloth
atop an uneven park bench.

It is Sunday, oversleeping church I have come
to atone in the warm dry grass, avoid chatter,
regroup from the weekday shuffle.
She watches me, a firmer version
of a younger self; I imagine pork ribs
soon to smolder on the aged grill,
cold potato salad in Tupperware,
the refreshing promise of a mason jar
holding sun tea with mint, a bit of South
in the Midwest.

• • •

She is a quaint nightmare, vagrant pilgrim
from my late-night despair: a grandmother
without grandchildren to scold, a mother
lacking sons to rotate the spit or fan smoke.
Like a child with a front seat to Punch and Judy,
I return a frosted smile, still afraid to taste her meat.

SHEREE RENÉE THOMAS

Lightning bug reflects

lightning bug reflects
a mason jar of silence
gold dust in my hand

The Reason I Know the Devil Is Mean

I know the devil is mean because
He vexes Sister Brown
Each and every third Sunday morning
When her solo comes around.

He sets her clock twenty minutes late,
Won't let her car start right.
He puts a frog off in her throat.
Oh, you wouldn't believe his spite!

But even if her sugar's low
Or if she's got a cold,
Sister Brown stands up third Sunday morning,
And gets that devil told.

"Y'all pray for me," she tells the church.
"I'm gonna do my best.
But Satan's got it out for me.
Won't let me get no rest."

And then she grabs aholt the mic
And sings her song real loud.
And when she finally takes her seat,
Her smile shows that she's proud.

And that's how I know the devil's no good,
That he's a low down dirty thing.
Spending his time on Flora Mae Brown
When heaven knows she can't sing.

Nat Turner in the Clearing

Ashes, Lord—
But warm still from the fire that cheered us,
Lighted us in this clearing where it seems
Scarcely an hour ago we feasted on
Burnt pig from our tormentor's unwilling
Bounty and charted the high purpose your
Word had launched us on. And now, my comrades
Dead, or taken; your servant, pressed by the
Bloody yelps of hounds, forsaken, save for
The stillness of the word that persists quivering
And breath-moist on his tongue: and these faint coals
Soon to be rushed to dying glow by the
Indifferent winds of miscarriage—What now,
My Lord? A priestess once, they say, could write
On leaves, unlock the time-bound spell of deeds
Undone. I let fall upon these pale remains
Your breath-moist word, preempt the winds, and give
Them now their one last glow, that some dark child
In time to come might pass this way and, in
This clearing, read and know.

JAYE FARREN

prelude to a new plague

marisol arrives in the wrinkled palm
of a gray-haired sunday morning /orange juice
turning sour on her tongue /as she talks about
how christians sometimes make gay people feel small
before swatting at them with church fans
advertising funeral homes //

for safety /we spend hours
turning the bars of the rainbow
into serpents / should doves swoop down
& try to peck us to death
while saintly calla lilies sound their trumpets
at a job well done //

Speaking in Tongues

for Camille

Remember the sanctuary:
you in a dress you had to wear
even when it wasn't Sunday,
me in the clipped-on navy blue tie
that put an itch in my neck
I still cannot scratch.
All we had to do was open
our mouths, and sure as the risen Savior,
He'd come through
lighting our tongues
with language.

Today, no one can beg you
back to the congregation
of fat men eager to shake your hand
while scratching your palm with an index finger
and crying women
who would sheet your knees
with a handkerchief as your legs grew
too long for your dress.
And I have forgotten both
the weight of a choir robe on my shoulders
and the fear of damnation
should my eyes confess
and meet those of a layman:
my clear falsetto
lost to a weak tenor.

• • •

Do you remember the sanctuary
and how we opened
our mouths for Him
to come through?

Today, you'd probably call Him
"Her," and I'd make some comment
about tonal languages, the ancestors,
spiritual connections—anything to explain
how we lost
our religion.

My Mother's Tornado

My mother says, *The tornado swept our field sideways.*
When she looks out from the porch
the boards of the shed torque towards buckle,
tomatoes bruise purple in the soil.

She says, *It hit like an atomic bomb.*
It was like the wind was made of pennies;
that's how much the air hurt.

My eyes—they are different seeds
than hers. She does not see
the chains holding the porch swing to the ceiling,
the chicks speeding their dust circles.

Honey, she insists, *the twister took the house down.*
But I heard the screen door slam
when I went to husk the corn out back.
And I have seen the fields shudder
before they know what spring will bring.

She says, *Do you want to hear how it was?*
I sit under a tree, staring west.
I hang onto my fistfuls of grass,
waiting for her storms to fallow,
for her memory to return to her a useful yield.

The seeds I set down uncurl slowly in the soil.
The air so still it does not complain
when it is forced out of the way.

Goodness and Mercy Shall Follow Me

I used to think about infinity for several minutes at a time, the hourglass on its side, the narrow neck breathing out into each chamber. Not having the faintest idea about how that would work, I always moved on to something I could wrap my mind around, like how loudly my stepfather snored when he was dog-tired, how people in my South sit on porches and front stoops like they're waiting for anything like heaven to be flung before their eyes, anything electric and mighty different. About porches and front stoops in heaven, I've yet to think long. But won't all those who make it be electric? Pure light filing before pure light? At rest in the neck of that same hourglass?

Goldsboro Narrative #20

That night at church camp, the boys' room packed
With bunk beds, when Vernon beseeched
Deliverance, I heard boys confess
They loved to smoke weed or drink Boone's Farm;

And when it was my turn, not loving either,
I said I wanted to be delivered from music.
Vernon laid his hands on me, saying, Lord,
Save this child from his sin. And I listened

For absence, my desire for my 45s to be gone.
I hadn't said what really bothered me.
And in the same way none of us spoke to be
Relieved of lust, I was worrying with my own

For a boy I lay near, caught up in the fever of fearing
What could happen. A Christmas before, I'd been given
A transistor radio, a small olive box with fake-wood paneling,
Tuned eternally to AM. I kept my radio with me

While I rode my bicycle; I listened to it as I washed dishes or
Cleaned up my room; I fell asleep with it near my head.
One night, its signal only hissed each time I clicked the radio on.
I prayed for sound to come back, and when it didn't

. . .

I felt foolish, tried drifting off into the usual night noise.
So it made sense to me that summer at eleven or twelve
To confess this folly to my new and older friends.
And I thought for a moment that, if I reminded myself

What lay hidden each night Vernon prayed over our souls,
I could finally be saved. And the absence within would dull
Rushes pouring through my chest whenever I looked for more
Than a glance at Millard, at Melvin, or at Bruce.

I would be unburdened of the very feeling lighting through
My body, that chance I would go straight to hell
The moment the world ended, the righteous gone up into air,
Me left on earth in all that silence.

Storm Named Earl

Wilmington, North Carolina

Years later a storm named Earl would come swinging
wind across this city named in 1730 for the Earl of Wilmington.

We called them storms then. When I was a kid, hurricanes
were named for girls, pretty girls like Hazel and Juanita.

Every year of those growing up years, rain heavy
as angry air pounded and pushed September into October

into the first few cold days of sad November. I remember
garbage cans and lids effortlessly flying down the street

sometimes drifting like dirty sheets of white notebook paper
beating down the coastline of my seaport pirate town.

Wind the size of titanic waves bounced the city farther
and farther inland. Outlets and inlets traded places

on the fear-laden faces of real estate beachfront property
ownership. But seasons here change as everywhere, I suppose.

Blue crab–catching season came in midJuly. Oyster season
always came in time to celebrate the thanks of giving.

. . .

You had to be careful driving at night during deer season
and nigger (known as coon season) was year round.

In this city where even today Niggerhead Road still
haunts the white center line, I came to love

the river sounds of Cape Fear. Catfish big as baby sharks
used to bite headlines off of newspapers used to wrap

up fish stories. Headlines like Negro boy arrested
for loitering around and about the New Hanover County Library.

I spent 29 and ½ days waiting for my social-status number
to be verified so I could check out a 75-cent paperback book.

I never returned it. Precisely what they were afraid of. I
proved the headlines right every night when forecasters

plotted the approach of another impending storm.
White people would board up their windows with ply board,

mask their faces with tape across storm-front doors, tie down
their yachts and garbage cans, stock up on flashlight

batteries and perishables and pray that all would be saved.
We never did any of this. The storm was just another god

and if he wanted to come into our home, we would let him
just as we let the downtown-sign-painting god hang

COLORED WAITING ROOM signs around our necks, just as
we let the bus-driving god direct us to sit in the rear, just

as we let the restaurant god tell us not to come in here, just
as we let the water-fountain god offer to us the coolest

•   •   •

drink of water on any Carolina hot summer day. I
can still hear my grandmamma saying: "If all we had to worry

about were storms . . ." Years later a storm named Earl would come
and the black people would tape up their own windows, but

I would be gone by then.

The Myth and Rumble of Memory
under the Hammer of Jeopardy

Harriet Tubman's Email 2 Master

(Subject: directions to the new place)

go
down past glass
ground in your salt shaker

make a right
between
arsenic sweet tea swallows

i am easy to find.
just take the fork where

mothers kill their babies
to keep them safe from you

and
look for
windows growing shotguns.

seven crown man

I am the seventh son of
a seventh son, the last one
a seventh son, the last one
my line comes from bless'd earth
my line comes from bless'd earth
a blueblack star marked my birth
I am the seventh son of

a blueblack star marked my birth
a razor blade cut my course
a razor blade cut my course
no one found the afterbirth
no one found the afterbirth
could be better, could be worse
a blueblack star marked my birth

could be better, could be worse
got what old folks call 'the touch'
got what old folks call 'the touch'
some men fight against their fate
some men fight against their fate
couldn't tote my blueblack weight
could be better, could be worse

• • •

couldn't tote my blueblack weight
or bend the notes so pretty
or bend the notes so pretty
my blues travels heavenbound
my blues travels heavenbound
men cry when they hear its sound
couldn't tote my blueblack weight

men cry when they hear its sound
brine and gin and Georgia clay
brine and gin and Georgia clay
one look makes grown women sin
one look makes grown women sin
my blueblack eyes, coal black skin
men cry when they hear its sound

my blueblack eyes, coal black skin
I pick up where he left off
I pick up where he left off
Night is mister mystery
Night is mister mystery
don't you try to look for me
my blueblack eyes, coal black skin

don't you try to look for me
I'll be gone come daybreak new
I'll be gone come daybreak new
wait and see, these bones fly free
wait and see, these bones fly free
seventh son of mystery
don't you try to look for me

"Seven Sevens" is a poetic form, created by Cave Canem instructor Kate Rushin,
consisting of stanzas of seven lines in a repeating pattern, with each line having seven
syllables. A poem of seven linked stanzas is called a "crown."

Reward

RUN AWAY from this sub-
scriber for the second time
are TWO NEGROES, viz. SMART,
an outlandish dark fellow

with his country marks
on his temples and bearing
the remarkable brand of my
name on his left breast, last

seen wearing an old ragged
negro cloth shirt and breeches
made of fearnought; also DIDO,
a likely yellow wench of a yellow

cast, born in cherrytime in this
parish, wearing a mixed colored
coat with a bundle of clothes,
mostly blue, under her good

arm. Both speak tolerable plain
English and may insist on being
called Cuffee and Khasa respect-
ively. Whoever shall deliver

.   .   .

the said goods to the gaoler
in Baton Rouge, or to the Sugar
House in the parish, shall receive
all reasonable charges plus

a genteel reward besides what
the law allows. In the mean
time all persons are strictly
forbid harbouring them, on pain

of being prosecuted to the utmost
rigour of the law. Ten guineas
will be paid to anyone who can
give intelligence of their being

harboured, employed, or enter-
tained by a white person upon
his sentence; five on conviction
of a black. All Masters of vessels

are warned against carrying them
out of state, as they may claim
to be free. If any of the above
Negroes return of their own

accord, they may still be for-
given by

ELIZABETH YOUNG.

J. W. RICHARDSON

The Politics of Breathing

You think you know me, but I'm barely breathing:
if you crack the door, you won't smell collards cooking,
just spilled buttermilk in a noon sun, seething;

and I'm not some Grendel, blue-black and heaving
over red, razor lips; blanched back, arched for fucking,
trying to *know* one who is barely breathing;

and I'm not on some page creased to heavy nigger pleading,
a pale, marbled shaft, some dark people sucking,
and spilled buttermilk in a noon sun, seething.

I stripped Mary naked—what I saw left me reeling:
dried shit, bone-dust—that's what I get for looking—
(you didn't tell me she wasn't even breathing);

I gouged a marble, blue-eyed Christ for peeping,
while all the blond lovelies, coon drunk, were hoofing
over spilled buttermilk in a noon sun, seething;

I aired out my lungs, hocked the phlegm, cursed the wheezing
thunder at my back, the Aloisius-shuffling
into shushing realms, realms barely breathing
spilled buttermilk
                              the noon sun

                                             seething.

We Are Not Responsible

We are not responsible for your lost or stolen relatives. We cannot guarantee your safety if you disobey our instructions. We do not endorse the causes or claims of people begging for handouts. We reserve the right to refuse service to anyone. Your ticket does not guarantee that we will honor your reservations. In order to facilitate our procedures, please limit your carrying on. Before taking off, please extinguish all smoldering resentments. If you cannot understand English, you will be moved out of the way. In the event of a loss, you'd better look out for yourself. Your insurance was cancelled because we can no longer handle your frightful claims. Our handlers lost your luggage and we are unable to find the key to your legal case. You were detained for interrogation because you fit the profile. You are not presumed to be innocent if the police have reason to suspect you are carrying a concealed wallet. It's not our fault you were born wearing a gang color. It is not our obligation to inform you of your rights. Step aside, please, while our officer inspects your bad attitude. You have no rights that we are bound to respect. Please remain calm, or we can't be held responsible for what happens to you.

The Good Funeral

after Stevie Smith

No one heard the dead man
        They were all too busy singing
And the son shouting *"daddy! daddy!"*—
        launching himself at the coffin
It took three men to wrestle him back
        so no one heard the dead man
the moans so softly lingering
        as if he were drowning but not yet gone—
that was   I think   why I heard him

Everyone loves a good funeral
        a hand-clapping   palm-waving funeral
a deep-singing   hard-crying funeral
        You leave full of fire and fried chicken
eyes red   head throbbing   happy somehow
        The dead man loved his good times too
Never to return

He was swimming and then he was drowning
        and the woman beside him had long been beside him
though not his wife they said
        A chill in his heart surprised him
cold creeping up from his toes to his chest
        And his wife at home they said

. . .

The widow is stolid   still
        face like a plate   wiped clean of care—
and Piedmont earth   six rectangular feet
        excavated from her chest
She is silent amid the singing
        She looks cold   her hands look cold
For it's never been warm enough   never
        So the dead are always saying—
though no one can hear for the singing

My Heart

Susan Smith has invented me because
Nobody else in town will do what
She needs me to do.
I mean: jump in an idling car
And drive off with two sad and
Frightened kids in the back.
Like a bad lover, she has given me a poisoned heart.
It pounds both our ribs, black, angry, nothing but business.
Since her fear is my blood
And her need part mythical,
Everything she says about me is true.

Hands, 1921

Silas's hands,
not the creamy brown
of hens' eggs
like his father's
or the red brown
of rust on a hoe
like Benjamin's
or the golden brown
of scuppernongs
on the vine
in late summer,
but the brown
of oak leaves
in late fall—
hog killing time,
hold open
The Life and Adventures
of Nat Love
Better Known
in Cattle Country
as Deadwood Dick
a man who has the hands
of a slave, a cowboy,
and a Pullman porter.

• • •

Love's hands,
not the brown
of tobacco leaves—
sun cured
hung in the smokehouse,
or the yellow brown
of a lariat
looped around
a longhorn's neck,
but the black brown
of crossties—
creosote soaked,
raise tobacco,
rope range cattle,
haul passenger baggage,
and at night caress
each other
lulled by the rustle
of callus against callus.

Wanderlust shines
in Love's eyes—
pennies tipped
to a Pullman porter—
drives him westward
to country hardly
held in history.

. . .

It is a grand sight
to see a large herd
of several thousand
buffalo on a stampede,
all running
with their heads down
and their tongues
hanging out
like red flannel,
snorting and bellowing
they crowd along,
shaking the ground
for yards around.

This is the answer
Love gives Silas as he
feels the train's approach
standing at the edge
of the track on the edge
of Milledgeville looking
on the rest of the world.

Drapery Factory, Gulfport, Mississippi, 1956

She made the trip daily, though
later she would not remember
how far to tell the grandchildren—
Better that way.
She could keep those miles
a secret, and her black face
and black hands, and the pink bottoms
of her black feet
a minor inconvenience.

She does remember the men
she worked for, and that often
she sat side by side
with white women, all of them
bent over, pushing into the hum
of machines, their right calves
tensed against the pedals.

Her lips tighten speaking
of quitting time when
the colored women filed out slowly
to have their purses checked,
the insides laid open and exposed
by the boss's hand.

• • •

But then she laughs
when she recalls the soiled Kotex
she saved, stuffed into a bag
in her purse, and Adam's look
on one white man's face, his hand
deep in knowledge.

Dinah in the Box

Dinah spent twenty hours with her face by the breathing hole, her body curled
like a nursing child's, wondering what order of thanks she would offer the man
who opened her crate. She had a particular trick that worked on Jennings
when she needed him to understand she meant to please, but Dinah wouldn't
be a bachelor's wench in Philadelphia. What angle would her legs take,
that first night in Philadelphia, in relation to the woman spot between them?
Not this infant's pose she was confined to now. Not any of the poses favored by Jennings.
What would her hands do, free to touch only what they chose? She had twenty hours
to remember every way she'd folded to get into this box. She'd tipped out extra brandy
until Jennings railed against the things he hated: taxes, drought, and abolitionists.
Turned out old Harrison, the carpenter, was suspected to be one. She tracked Harrison
and asked what price and means he'd name. Those two tasks proved more simple
than storing up the coins that slipped from Jennings' pocket to the rug beside the bed.
It took Dinah seven months to collect enough to buy the box and pay Harrison
for the bill of lading. Dinah touched her knees, tracing the hinge inside them
that would straighten in some white man's parlor. She wasn't free yet, but soon
a man she would make herself trust would prize open the lid of her crate.

reply to grandma taylor

b. early 1800s, Willington, South Carolina

i sew a cord
navel to dust
blood to dreams
spit to endings

circling the horizon
time without end

i call our names anew

with these hands
i become a weaver of space

a rod divining the soil of my tomorrows
cutting lines into an earthen path

that rain will turn to mud

that sun will dry into steps

that children seeking freedom will walk
into the center of their own one heart

. . .

i roll oil over the skull
worm between light and shadows

singing because

somewhere
a road is still wet with the blood of truth

somewhere
a pain is matching my own

somewhere
i have already sung

the kelley women: a story of africans and romas

my mother was afraid of romas
whenever she encountered the parlors
with the tinted signs   tarots read here   or
a pink neon handprint etched with blue lettering
proclaiming madam z cures afflictions
and removes jumbies from any dwelling
she'd remind me of her rearing up
in kilmarnock and the "gypsies" as she puts it
would camp out on their land with tents
boiling cauldrons, rickety trucks carrying
loads of roma-essence. they preferred to camp out
back along the flower fairies and tree lilies
mz cinda had instilled fear   what kind of white
folks camp on a colored person's land. by this
time the kelley men had long left no traces of
manhood or folk men about the place   my mother and
her mother mae would peep about the encampment
when the romas went to town to sell fortunes
the fortune-tellers were a threat to those who believed in jesus and hoodoo
they feared their spells may have more strength than the african
obeah but the dark hair and the dark white skin my mother said
could be a sign of colored influence   mz cinda reckoned these spell
    makers
may be weaker because of this miscegenated power but they "beared"
    watching
my mother bea   mae's daughter found a strange colored doll which they
attempted to give in friendship but history taught her "different"
no   they "beared" watching from the house up by the road
just in case

Mississippi Gardens

slaves, she answers. as I sink
my fingers beneath the roots.

the knees of that blue housedress are threadbare.
she wears it on Tuesdays and Fridays when we tend the flowers.

pullin' weeds ain't a time for talk she chides.
I watch her uproot the creeping charlie.

the fragrant blossoms we protect, hug our whole house.
sweet peas were my choice.

we rarely buy those things for sale in the gardening aisle.
don't make sense to work the earth and not feel it.

I wanted those thick cotton gloves, but they stayed on the shelf.
you gotta learn the difference between dirt and soil.

sometimes I notice how the ground changes.

denser, darker, moister a little more red in some places

in social studies class I learned about crop rotation

and how it keeps the land fertile.

Mama, what did they used to grow here?

Southland

"In the land of cotton
old times there
are not forgotten
look away . . ."

Booker T, son of ole virginy
wanders around in the coal mine
he is afraid   *(sinner, please don't let this harvest pass)*
he is looking for a podium
a hoe and a match
a match a hoe and a podium
gotta got to gotta
school invisible (wo)men on
how to game their
way into the academy in
one long stroke
                          (pause here for minstrel interlude)
imagine there's no heaven
just melting clocks
on barren fields that ragtime Toomer
willed to Gurdjieff or ragtime Gurdjieff willed to Toomer.
passing Little Buckland,
I think I spy him in the cottonfield
"Booker, is that you?"
practicing how he will say

• • •

"O Lawd, de cotton am so grassy,
de work am so hard, and the sun am so hot
dat I b'lieve dis darky am called to preach!"
the magic words for making and unmaking
"most black, brother, most black"

Off to see the Wizard
I turn off the highway
and there is he
behind the shotgun house in
block-back coat and Stetson hat
helping Trueblood get his lie straight:

Wizard: Now when they ask you were you there, what are you going to
             say?
Trueblood: I cannot tell a lie. I was there, but sometimes it causes me to
             tremble, tremble, tremble.
Wizard: That won't do. Won't do.
Trueblood: Then what I'm sposed to say, Chief?
Wizard: "I have not been successful in securing any information that
             would throw any accurate light . . ."
but Du Bois interrupts from the porch
to grouse about fractions.
he tells us we are divided against ourselves.

somebody's playin Gershwin so sweetly.
it ain't necessarily so and so—
I catch my mouth disappearing
as an involuntary "yassuh" slips out *hissssss*
to carress
some distinct dude
who volunteers to split the tab
for history's sake.
I demure.

. . .

says he: "What we have is a failure to communicate"
says I: "We can't all get along,"
but sweetly, in the key of
"Roll Jordan Roll / Roll Jordan Roll / I want
to go to heaven when I die / to see old Jordan roll
over.

Sometimes I (dis)remember things, too.
Lincoln Perry played Stepin Fetchit
Jesse B. Semple played himself

(Do nothing till you hear from me)

Gershwin was making some headway,
but he dissolved into some
Monkish stuff with piano, saxophone, and bass.

later, "the day the music died" posthaste
they had not consulted me
and some blues prints.
they were singing
"bye bye miss American pie"
I could have told them Elvis is not dead yet,
but I couldn't catch rye on the levee
with the good old boys.

My sisters advised me to imbibe
heavy doses of oliver lake
nina simone k.d. lang aretha miles
dvořák
then find a brother or sister
who could help me
come
        to

            terms.

my brother thinks
I have rubbed my head
against the Jericho walls of (drums please)
edu(my)cation for so long for so long for so long
that I have
mis-termed the struggle
my mind a blackbo(a)rd
                     with inscription
(Take me to da water, or
take me tu da wadder, or
tek me tad a wata ohyesohyes)
consider Mr. Brown's sterling decoding
system
to determine
which one is correc'.
little neo/colored girls still lament
nappy edges
though dark and lovely can burn
all trace of Africa
from the temple,
leaving shiny bald skin in its place.
is it, "who be ye" or
"who you be?"
the answer lay festering in a (w)hole
note knotted until
it showed up unannounced
on the mid-Atlantic shore,
then, resurfaced in New England pews
or exquisite South Carolina grill work.

. . .

News of this marvel traveled
by way of Jacob's ladder   (*every round goes higher, higher*)
The answer waded in the water,
pushed through a hole,
till it was worn into itself.
The answer swam to shore with Shine
(*whose light is a-comin*)
Oh, rise, Shine—
Coltrane blows sweetly over the Carolinas
supreme love
how we be—
(*you can play Dixie right here*)
do we be . . .
we be (*play john lee hooker here*)
do we be . . .
we be (*play bessie and mamie and billie*)
we be? (*play coltrane and pharaoh and the sonny's*)
(*Play sweet honey in the rock*)
we be . . . we be . . . we be . . . we be . . .
webewebewebewebewebewebe
drums

On The Road

Imagine you wake up with
A second chance: Silent evening
Wider than tomorrow, the breeze
Like a kiss from heaven. Tired out
From work, but you don't mind
The walk. Still, an offered ride
Is welcome.

At what point does the road narrow, turn?
When do the minds beside you
Unmask themselves? Do their eyes reflect
White hoods before or after you are
Beaten? Between the kicks? Before or
After you are chained to a
Rust-pocked bumper?

If you don't look back the future
Never happens: the road does not rise
To meet your broken face, the
Last taste in your mouth is honeydew,
Not your blood and fear. *The whole sky is yours.*

Funny what the mind will focus on:
A silent calf standing in a field.
The blink of fireflies.
The way your left leg twists
Back onto itself. The dented license plate,
The last thing of this world you will see.

• • •

Imagine you wake up with
A second chance.
Imagine
You wake up.

Italicized lines from "Dawn Revisited" by Rita Dove.

redemption lullaby 2

1
if you close your eyes
tight really tight
hold them still
they will come
the women who look
just like you
but older
older than stone
older than water
older than air
dancing in circles of fire
lifting the fire
above their heads
like hallelujah bonnets
shaping twisting bending
fire into scarves skirts
pregnant bellies.

• • •

2
if you close your eyes
tight really tight
hold them still
you will come to yourself
learn to lift your own fire
in mirrors of ocean
learn to scold the smile
the heat that steals your face
locks out husbands
sons lovers fathers
howls at clocks
whose hands
have forgotten to strike.

3
you reclaim face heat
rename the fire
as you strangle women
who lift bend twist
your tongue
in this newness
the fire renames
your face
swallows all your names
eats your skirts
your pillows your bed

we sleep now eyes wide open painted red.

Clay

Joe Frazier remembers Madison Square Garden, March 8, 1971

red clay bruiser with nigger brag, he could dance, now,
'round Vietnam, & for his honorable divisible nation.

Clay was always Tomming somebody out. MLK was a Tom.
Jesus was a Tom. & hot sauce chitlin' swine was Tom food.

more *as-salaam alaikum* than an ex-con on a corner,
he was Cassius, pretty Ali—legend of a man.

showed up at the garden with his red trunks
and a mouth fulla two-fisted fight,

and me in the green trunks, facing it down,
not there to be right about nothing, but in it to win.

way i saw it, i was a man with two choices:
lose the fight or whup Clay's ass.

couldn't go down like no sucker, either. so i battled.
eleventh round, it all started to run together:

bells-grease-left jab-right uppercut-winner-loser—
a wide-eyed world droning in the bloat.

his feet tapped Bojangles like soft-shoe,
blood from us both spilling Aunt Jemima red.

Spring 1937

for Honoré Roussel

the fullmoon night hog maws fell
from heaven and pigs knuckles exploded
like bombed crackers in the bloom
of our prized magnolia

the night you lay waked all resplendent
in smooth depression serge
and pennypinch satin
your cold horizontalism
fronting the fireplace plugged
against troublesome swifts
paralleling the close ragtime piano
locked and draped
as though it might otherwise play
insolently of its own accord

that fateful night of the evergreen sprig
in the sprinkling holywater clutches
of the mournful faithful
and their cascading hail marys

• • •

was the night of the mysterious maws
come rain and thunder tumbling
from an invisible sky
spangling a multivoiced presence
in the crest of our featured magnolia
that sang you to an explosive levitation

shattering the plugged fireplace
unmasking the hooded piano
scattering mourners like sootwinged swifts
like rag feathered notes
through corridors rooms and chinks
of your wintered house.

Nosotros

escuchame amigo
I used to be you
raking, cleaning
picking, mucking, shining
grinning, dreaming
almost invisible
to the people you serve

mis vatos
I used to be you
In the back corner of the classroom
engulfed in your own silence
waiting patiently for the curriculum
to acknowledge your existence
outside of your unico dia, your
cinco de mayo
to raise you above a stereotype
to speak to you with your own tongue

hermanas bonitas
I used to be you
attempting to hide behind oppressive
accents and grammar rules
surrendering to the Gap
settling for color-lessness
after discovering invisibility is imposible
and peroxide and French perfume
won't hide the Rio Bravo in your smile

. . .

mi gente
somos lo mismo tu y yo
necesito decirte
cherish who you are y tu familia
ama el café of your eyes
love your nose and face
learn from my mistakes

Laughing Strong

They grew
laughing black men
out of Missouri dirt
like Nebraska corn.

They grew men
who laughed
as tall as California
redwoods.

Now that I have
my own baby man
I need to know
how they did it.

Cause this world sure
ain't funny.

Grandma Mary begat
Bee-at, who begat Uncle Son
and Chuck, who begat Robbie,
Ray, Lan and Dee.

All good laughing
black men.
Do not mistake
my meaning.

• • •

I ain't talking
bout no sell out
chuckle.
This is living laughter.

The kind
that creates
warmth where
there is none.

These men are
hurt your gut
choke on your water
wipe your eyes funny.

How do you make
a keep going
keep laughing
black man?

One day after
his close friend
dies in Iraq,
my brother

has us laughing
until we ache.
Mama,
how did you do that?

How did you teach him
to throw jokes and not
punches? To swallow
laughs and not drinks.

What is the laughing black man recipe?

between witches

listen.

you must refrain from coming here
until after the sun
has lowered
into the mouth of a mountain.

wait two hours
& remember to wear your cloak
the one we snatched off the night's bones
eve of winter solstice.

i am convinced the neighbors spotted us
making nice with the shadows
breastfeeding the hungry ghosts
of all the daughters
who died before being born.

police have been pounding at my door
twice yesterday
& a total of ten times this summer
frightening moths
shattering the bulbs of fireflies
causing the hairy-legged crickets
& bearded irises
shaving in the front yard
to cut themselves.

. . .

spiders are looking for a new place
to hold their meetings
so they can roast beetle
& share web-spinning secrets
without the fear of slaughter.

even the spell books
that used to sit on the kitchen table
are now hidden under the stairs
next to the cauldrons
where they snort dust to dull the anger.

until nature deems it safe again
we shall make magic a different way
be like the artisan witches of paris
& copenhagen:

paint colorful stars on each other's back
& pray they become constellations.

SHARAN STRANGE

Claim

My tongue, every atom of my blood, form'd from this soil, this air,
Born here of parents born here from parents the same, and their parents the same . . .
— *Walt Whitman*

Sun reaching through the bus window makes her a flame.
White cloth twining her head ignites the tip of a body
Dressed all in white, as if readied for dipping in the Sunday stream,

Though she hardly knew the woman who would have counseled
Her preparation—reminding her not to fight the preacher, just
Lay back, meet the water with the ease of the unburdened—

Who had left these backwoods, dispossessed and angry,
By this same road but northward, like ancestors
Who traced rivers, moss, nocturnal light to the city.

This trip reverses that repudiation of the South.
As she recounts her grandmother's deathbed wishes and
Reviews her own bitter struggles, she's a torch

Glowering in midday. Old cruelties mark this soil.
Its memory takes trope in jolts her crippled back records,
And she winces, reminded of a new corporate toll.

But a disability settlement's reluctant reparation
Is just enough to purchase her inheritance,
Make her the family's agent fulfilling old ambition.

. . .

Gnarled braids escape her headwrap, signify on native trees
Warped by heavy fruit. The house those trees built—
Taproots drawing her forebears' blood and sweat, their cries,

And prayers into the very walls—will be her grandmother's again.
The Greyhound's bringing their twinned spirits home,
Where she'll make for them an unassailable shrine.

DURIEL E. HARRIS

specimen

The bringing	
of the	total
African to America	imported
planted	into
the	North
the first seed of	America
	Estimated percent of
dis-Union.	total[1]
The bringing	
. . .	. . .

Sources: D. W. Griffith, *Birth of a Nation*, 1915, title card. Todd Savitt, *Medicine and Slavery* (Urbana, Illinois, 2002 [1978, 1981]), 32.

mulcted
a literal sea, banquet
of bodies: good ore, plenty filling
our ministrations' delicious martyrdom

to harvest curative measures
we, the great house, procure
(pox and fever catalogue)
blank black cadavers at derelict speed

in hospital, a prayerful negro
congregation, malingering—of course
makes for robust anatomical dough
to raze a proper contagion

• • •

i.e. case [Jefferson to Waterhouse, 21 August 1801]
cultivated pustules—putrid scabs' soft seepage
—evict—puns evince—living pox
(glee:

> *The Negress Sarah, a cook, had been injected with fresh matter and took*
> *the infection mildly. A later introduction proved uneventful;*
> *our experiment, a success.*

chocolatey dessert
and brandy to aid digestion)

[1] Senegambia	13.3
Sierra Leone	5.5
Winward Coast	11.4
Gold Coast	15.9
Bight of Benin	4.3
Bight of Biafra	23.3
Angola	24.5
Mozambique-Madagascar	1.6
Unknown	0.2
Total	100.0

In the Company of Women

my first feminists lived on 131st street &
kinsmen in cleveland / sported big bangle hoop
earrings / fly feathered doos w/ tails in back & freshly
pressed sergio valente's for picture day

nobody tried to quiet they voice
no one could misinterpret head angled on a down
slope / forefinger pointing up / as a homegirl say
um excuse you / you best be stepping off

off the runways of the ghetto
they were the women i wanted to be
with names like / lanita / jerita / shondra
& monique / these cornrow fake louis vuitton big
booty wearing grape blow pop smacking kick
ball playing wash cars on saturday black & proud
spitting out nigga pleazes & show you rights
like it ain't a thang

my name is keisha
yeah
they call me boo
yeah
i am a leo
yeah
my man is desi
yeah
let's set it out

. . .

you were the women
could've been from anywhere / cute / cool & conversating
on classroom corners as
street lamps heat much
jheri curl juice to the sounds of / my
A-DI-DAS / defining you selves
w/ might on tongues in traditions of
davis / giovanni / & / shange

you were the women
the women i wanted to be
owning your world
double dutching into tomorrow
these words stand on playgrounds
in your memory / may your ears
rock to their beat

Fountain

I think first of thirst,—
not the lighted sprays sprinkling
domes of mist
over the small pond in my
gated community,
but of skin—
of black and white photographs,
public drinking fountains
labeled   COLORED   WHITES—

of what my mother could quench
in her time and what
she could not touch.
And of the phone call
I made to her from college
my freshman year.
A history class at
Washington and Lee
taught the origins of
the sit-in movement—
segregated lunch counters
at North Carolina A&T.

    • • •

You were there, I accused.
I had done the math
and it placed her
there, a freshman like me.
You never said anything
to us about it.

What is there to say about people
spitting in your food?
she demanded. And I remember
how, once, enraged, she spat
at me, my siblings, *Your lives have been*
what I've told you they've been
whether it was the truth
or not.

She has been gone two years.
Outside, uncounted
droplets from the fountain
hit the pond.
I stand inside at my window
and watch. My life
is this recording.

Chaperone on the Chicago Charter

1 /
I've become that woman at the front
of the bus. The one with mints and tissue
who watches things,
saves seats.

No more need to clamor
for the bench at the back, the aisle
of whispers and smoky looks.
I go for the support of a sturdier chair—

the modest recline, the easy egress,
the view of the wide road ahead.

2 /
Someone starts a sing-along,
a cappella version of something
I don't know by someone
I don't recognize

but want so much to sing.
It rises from the rear, like ballgame
cheer, this new song, this code.
Where have I been

while all of this was going on?

Outside of my window—other buses,
other windows, other women in the front.

• • •

3 /
They leave everything
when it is time to get off.

Empty cups with two straws each.
Hamburger wrappings.
Dead batteries.
A single silver earring.
None of them are mine
to gather.

This is what I came with:
a book of poems, some fruit,
a silent phone.

What's new is this chill in the night.
Not my stars to claim, but still—

West of Dawn

I
Bendullah
pushes
a push mower
before him
pulls a lawn mower
behind him
walks west
of dawn

He crosses the Choptank
to Talbot County,
where rich white folks
pay him crisp loot
a cold glass of water
to manicure their blue grass

His real name
is Ben Chase
so my aunt says
some kin
to Sherman-Chase-the-younger
who shot Gordon Briggs
in the throat with a .22

* * *

II
Bendullah walks
starlight to starlight
Mom says he gets
around better
than she does
and she has a car
All the men say,
he is strong, very strong
The brothers
who go for bad
don't jive
with him
only speak
about him
in whispers
When he passes,
there is silence
always

III
I saw Bendullah once
wipe sweat from his brow
with a blue cotton bandana
That was the only time
I saw his eyes
startled
like a deer's
He rested his right foot
on back a mower
slipped bandana
from his left pocket
folded and pressed it
against his glistening

He looked around, saw
me passing in my mom's 1956 Ford,
Saw a child wondering why
no one ever gave him a ride
just because he lived in a ghost
house with no paint, no windows
no running water
on a dirt road
down from "Praise the Lord"
Great Mt. Zion Holiness Church

IV
Uncle Norwood was the only
one gave Bendullah a ride
talked to him

Grandmom would say,
"You better let him walk."
My uncle would say,
"Hush, woman. You don't know
what you're talking about."
And my grandmother would say,
"Everybody knows what I talk about.
Bendullah axed his wife's head off.
One cut.
Clean through.
And they sent him up
The Chesapeake for it."

Bendullah
walks west.

Frederick Douglass to Three Young Men, Waiting

Do not stand beneath the live oak tonight.
Men like you should rage, rage against the wrong.
Rage, rage against the rope-burned limbs and fight!

As wise young men you must not yield to fright.
With powerful fists make a freedom gong.
Do not stand beneath the live oak tonight.

Men arm yourselves against the hooded knights.
The outcome you desire won't take too long.
Be encouraged, run from darkness to light.

You inhabit land about to ignite
in murder, mayhem, to kill freedom's song.
Do not stand beneath the live oak tonight.

A whip-poor-will sings its warning: midnight.
Find the cacodemon, join the throng.
Rage, rage against the rope-burned limbs and fight!

Sinister place of bloody roots invites
a response; bear arms, and battle the strong.
Do not stand beneath the live oak tonight.
Rage, rage against the rope-burned limbs and fight!

Resurrection under the Moon

But it be a gift, a gift
Out of they misery
I become blacker than the skin
of a tree in the rain,
and I be rooted
in the rich black earth.
Out of me flies the swallow.
— Dolores Kendrick, *The Women of Plums*

I wait in the sugarcane fields.
We meet under the moon's watch.
He look tired and worn
like a walking corpse.

He hurtin' bad. Master made sure
he made his point.
Slashed engravements traveling
like serpents, raisin' his skin with welts.

He walk up to me cautiouslike,
stare me right in the eyes
and somethin' in him come back to life.

He touch my hips,
like he can't believe they real.

• • •

My dress, I sews myself, he take apart,
real careful with each string and stitch,
like it be some fine tapestry.

He whisper my name over and over,
fearin' he might never speak it again.
You can tell how much a man love you
by the way he say your name.

He holds my name tight with his voice, tracin'
every syllable with his tongue, lettin'
it linger on his lips like watermelon wine.

All the while he be memorizing my eyes
Like he afraid he gon' forget the color.

The smell of my perfume,
my own potion of rose water and lily
with my work sweat and steam
from the hot water cornbread, bring him
back to the living world.

I tells him to lean on me, his back broken,
legs wilting like old oak branches.

I reach for his scent coiled tight to his head,
caress the plains of his shoulders.
I smell the young in him, hiding from master
and the whip, kept quiet in the pockets of his neck.

We link together, coming so close
our skin begins to melt.
His kisses brush my face like magnolia petals.

. . .

There ain't no room for fear when we
lovin' each other, this ain't for the takin',
rapin', and slavin',
master can't have this part of us.

I let him love me all night. I know
my lovin' keep him from the slave grave.

Black woman's love ain't nothin' casual.
Our love brings our men back from the dead.

Five

    black men
        spun like tops. Temptations
            that died in unison
                under Alabama sun,

    tangled together on lines
        spooled around the same tree—
                  fresh catch.

I wish
    they could've hummed to heaven

instead of being hooked   then flung there.

HOUSTON BAKER JR.

Another Man . . .

Chill sunlight
Catches rusted corrugations,
Bent tin, rotting timbers,
That were home, resonant on Sunday
With John's guitar in a second room.
Porch collapsed last year in sunbleached pile,
Weathered remains are like bones from time long dead.
A vision of stones in old fields,
Sorrel and toadflax repossessing the pasture,
Greets her this dawn.
Already smoke billows from the new brick chimneys,
Settles on brown sedge by the road.

Fall's frost found her unprepared for news of John:
Lost appeals and last-ditch failure, and
Today, deep South of here,
They will push a needle into his arm,
Pump poison till he's dead.
She inhales sweet gum, dusty like dried blood,
And thinks . . .

Lawd, have mercy
Mercy on me . . .

You Made Me

Out of the sanctity of old names,
birth & death cries, the transfigured
future crawls forth on two legs,
like the nine-headed beast
with a question in each eye.
It comes to us, a part of us,
beckoning Old Man River
dragging up earth to the slow mouth
of ragged song & surrender,
in quest, rage & prayer.
Mississippi John Hurt, Johnny
Cash, Big Mama Thornton, B. B.
King, Merle Haggard, the Carter
Family, Son House, Jerry Lee
Lewis, Bessie Smith, Professor Longhair—
roll call & September storm. The past
rises in red bud & bluejay, in blood oath
& ten ways to love a woman
or man. Out of the shapechanger's
lament, my burdened voice unearthed
in mid-sentence—"way down
in Egyptland" lives alongside
the leap-year's makada. The ghosts
at Shiloh Church trade tongues
with sexual lilies besides a millpond,
begging dumb-struck nights & taproot
into the blackest soil this side
of the Mason-Dixon. Out of this
wounded love squinting up
at the Southern Cross

above the Yellow Dog,
singing "Ezekiel saw the wheel"
as someone balled the jack
in a room at least a mile
inside a lonely house. I rise
beyond borrowed blame & the thing
turned inside out—caught
in the hinged jaw of love & hate,
I come forth. Out of good will,
I ride the waves of summertime
till I am back washing the midnight
blue out of work clothes
& Sunday-go-to-meeting suits
& dresses. I am man & woman,
daughter & son, an albino
in thirty-three shades of moonlight
beneath the last chinaberry tree.
Out of would-be kings
among Greek columns & facades
overlooking sharecropper shacks,
singled out & strung up
between tradition & live oak—
worm-hunger at the roots of the
Crosstree. I am a man
who came as a boy
out of Little Rock, Selma,
Mobile & Bogalusa.
Out of a land pregnant
with Indian mounds,
we newcomers stumble
out of English brogans, clod-
hoppers & wooden shoes
shaped like miniature boats.
Out of Sandy Hook,
blood ran into the law
of hands & the fruit
forcing branches to bow
over the graves. The worm

begat the mocking bird,
the mocking bird begat the one-eyed horse,
& the horse begat the idea of man
& woman. Out of frog holler,
love moans, birds of paradise
beside the hand pump
dragging up cool waters
from bedrock, I come
when you call my name
in a Wednesday night
prayer meeting or field
holler at daybreak.
Out of *Birth of a Nation*
& *Gone with the Wind*
a new cry owns the hills
& bank of the Tallahatchie.
I found Shango sitting beneath
a crab apple tree, holding a scorpion
on his palm. The herb man's medicine
had the bossman walking the floor
for seven nights as the two-headed
desire in my body worked
its way out of the blood
in this earth, red leaves
on the edge of an almost forgotten
season. Up from lowlands
to Blue Ridge & Stone Mountain,
our shadows face each other, one
divided into the other: the good
& the bad, this side of the brain
straddling the hex sign drawn
in Louisiana dirt. Out of this—
out of spit & mud, straw
& myth, catgut, love
& doubt, still I sing
till the auctioned-off faces
rise out of the bottomland.
There are no more marks

of ownership on my skin,
no secret kisses & hugs
to pull me under the hush
of white satin & lallygag
of reeds beside the still waters.

The Hush and Holler Portraits

Elegy For an Older Brother, 1922

Benny's handsome, red brown like rust on a hoe. Empty
headed cows loll in the pasture ignoring the mule's bray.
Light shines as easily through a cicada's husk clinging to a tree

as through a bottle of liniment or a glass of tea
on the dinner table. The hems of his overalls fray
and tickle Benny's skin as he plows. Empty

promises from a brother, emptied simply,
without volition, friable as leaves underfoot on a fall day,
translucent as a cicada's husk clinging to a tree.

Benny went to war across the water, over the sea.
He left himself here, on this side, on the quay.
Benny's thin and red brown like rust on a hoe. Empty

handed, back from France, he speaks of Paree
often, though he's been home three years come late May.
The day is empty like a cicada's husk clinging to a tree,

empty like sound after the mule's kick when Benny falls, free
of this place, then the hum of a bee and cry of a jay.
Benny's skin red brown like rust on a hoe is empty
as a cicada's husk clinging to a tree.

Like Father

My father's embrace is tighter
now that he knows
he is the only man in my life.
He whispers *remember when* and *I love you*
and holds my hand, hungry
for a discussion of Bible scriptures
over breakfast. We are like a cup of coffee
I won't stop spilling.

My father's embrace is firm and warm
now that he knows. He begs forgiveness
for anything he may have done to make me
turn
to abomination
as he watches my eggs, scrambled
soft. Yolk runs all over the plate.
A rubber band binds
the unopened morning paper.

My father's embrace tightens. Grits
stiffen. I hug back
like a little boy, gripping
to prove his handshake.
Daddy squeezes me close,
but I cannot feel his heartbeat
and he cannot feel mine—
there is too much flesh between us,
two men in love.

Sanctuary

for William Faulkner and my father, Earnest McEwen Jr.

Between the brush of angels' wings
and furious hooves of hell, two mortal men
fell down. How you must have looked—
white shirt stained, khakis fatigued,
smelling of sweat and smoke,
hair at odds with itself and the world.
At the threshold among your restless dead
in echo and shadow of ancient oaks,
providing sanctuary, offering shade,
you had many worlds behind you,
few yet to be born: stories of insurgence,
scorn, decay—theme and variations
of a vanquished South.

Leaning against a jamb
of antebellum brass, you watched, waited,
raised weary arm and hand, saluted
the familiar stranger. *Come. Enter. Sit. Sing.*

You reached each other across the grate.
What you two must have known of heaven and hell.

William Faulkner was my father's benefactor, paying for him to attend college at a
time when my father had little hope of earning enough money to pay for college
himself.

Some Are Dead and Some Are Living

ima gonna tattoo me on you for ever
leave my creases inside you creases
— Sonia Sanchez

1. Senesta
St. Louis evenings spoiling under electric lights
We leaned out the window above the tavern roof.
Her name better than any song on the juke box.
I'd say: Senesta, Look! That one and That
The sights male and musk: new smells inside some
Teenage fantasy and no one more surprised
Than us when the answer—deep as Wardell's
Cool bass jazz—floated up through the window
And grabbed us by the scruff. Left us feeling bad as any tough girl
Worse even—knowing we could never be.
And the lights flickering *Bud Bud Budweiser*
And the night inching toward dawn
And the two of us hanging forever over the sill.

. . .

2. Kay Frances

Led that prairie town around by the nose she did
As if her tar paper house wasn't built right
On Kansas tracks and kinky hair wasn't a dead give away
Even with light skin, grey eyes, and all.
She was townie queen and I rose to her summons, floating
With the others from college across double iron rails.
Left me singing: *Don't the moon look lonesome*
When passing trains rattled the wallpaper pattern
And I pretended not to hear the Great Northern
Or Eastern Flyer shaking coffee cups filled with gin
While bidwhist plays danced on the Naugahyde table.
Ice cubes slammed against my teeth like home runs
And mulatto-boned Kay behind a sweet curtsy smile
Watched me play, shivering in the tunnel of sounds.

3. Margaret

No doubt we always thought of leaving
That town reeking of beef on the hoof
The heel and toe of rundown cowboy boots
12th and Vine littered in bad blues.
We said we had plans to cross more lines
Than the packing house bridge separating states.
We wanted to make it big in some place
Where colors meant more than they appeared
And prairies were no more permanent than celluloid.
Now I hear pregnant with baby boys you turned
Almost religious—could have sworn—nearly did
After I skipped town singing: "Rocky Raccoon."
I held your voice miles away and that last
Phone call so far so close to my ear.

.   .   .

4. Snow

Behind your back we said it was your attitude
But something more elusive made us marvel
At the stance you took, feet toed out and ready
With the part of you that was hoodlum trapped
In a crazy mix of caprice and avarice.
If there had been tracks down the middle
Of this town, I would have met you crossing
And no matter what, asked whether
I was going the wrong way—Let me guess
You never needed anyone to tell you
It's tough out here and nobody dared
Call you half-pint even with that gravelly
Voice and nail hard way you don't touch, your skin
Velvet shadows as we reach and you turn away.

5. Toni Cade

Even when I tell you Seattle rolls up
At midnight you won't take no for an answer.
Hell, you couldn't take no for a question.
So we drive miles for the sake of Ethiopian
Cowpeas, kifto, and spongy bread served
Under fading posters of drylongso countries.
By word of mouth we stay alive, you say
Out here, you say, justice wears a newspaper hat
A single word in print dissolves whole families.
Over your shoulder, sidama stones rise from a poster.
We talk about moods and shrugs and why paths cross.
It's the stories, you say, the stories and I watch
You wet your finger in a bowl of rough salt
Lick it clean and say: Sometimes even this is sweet.

. . .

6. Jennie

Perhaps in your half-sleep world
You are still dancing in the living room
Rug thrown back to the quick kiss
Of your feet on bare wood floors.
Perhaps each visit merely interrupts
A day you remember best wordless
Behind the slow flutter of eyelids.
Perhaps you still guide us half-grown
Girls through hours of etiquette on how
To pour the proper rise of champagne
In water glasses or how right to find
Four leaves on clover growing in gutters.
Perhaps sweet Auntie the moon you taught me
To dream is still lovely and you remember to believe.

7. Fingerprints

Marked by a time when there were sidewalk games
And boundaries of the heart and home, we broke
Rules: *don't cross the tracks, step on the cracks.*
What our mothers didn't know didn't hurt them.
We grew like Topsy into women, no roads to pave
Our way, no looking back. I'd like to say we never
Attended to skin color, slapping palms for Mary Mack
Pick-up sticks and Jacks. I'd like to say I recall
Your faces clear as the day I tore my seersucker dress
Climbing a fence or took my first kiss under a night
Sky full of fireflies. I need to tell you this:
How memory served up in bits and pieces and yesterdays
Becomes so déjà-vu, I swear I almost see all of you
Standing there in the corner of the room.

Porch Monkey

She has no desire. She has a ring,
a ring on her hand that she twists
and twists again. She has a word,
one word in her chest that pushes
its way on an ache of air to her tongue.
But she does not speak it, will not
say its name. Here where she sits
she cannot see the corn spreading its arms

twisting its way up the rope
of the sun or the cotton's brazen
white blooms. She cannot see the men
in the field or the stone from the field
they were clearing. So many stones:
egg white, flinty grey, pink-flecked,
sun-warmed, black with blood.
There were three shotgun blasts from the field

that day. For the women at the well
it was a signal they knew, like a rattler's
hiss from the deeps of the hawthorn
thicket, and they hurried away. She stood
dreaming at the hand crank, listening
to the bucket suspended below,
the creak of hemp, the plash of thick water
clover honey brown, and the flies

. . .

bottle blue and thick as her thumb,
buzzing loud as mowers. Later
they told her what happened to Sweet,
his fall from the wagon, the stone arching
to meet him, how no one moved, then all
moved at once. They told her this those
hard men, faces and hands of tree
bark, tears standing in their leaf brown eyes.

Now it is she who does not move.
She's ill, they tell her. They do not
make her work, slap her hands
from the biscuit dough, say she'll curdle
the milk in the churn. She spends her
afternoons on the porch where the wind
in the pines seems a live thing bent
on thrashing all the mockingbirds

and whippoorwills from their nests.
They complain so loudly the voice
of the child at her knee disappears—
disappears into the radio's buzz, the low
songs of women, disappears
into the scraping of cicadas,
the hot, hot tongue of longing—
the sun.

Mississippi Fretless

Neck smooth
as rosewood
earrings black

tuning my hands
turning my hands
tremble at the

tension round
midnight, earlobes
and Mississippi delta.

I am eyes closed
in her rhythm
changes and I

have to get the
moves right and
it has to be fretless.

Her voice is
made for
moonlight.

Her dress is
nothing but
a glaze.

•   •   •

Help me Jaco.
Help me Jesus
hold her as I should—

improvise, resonate
swing, till every note
speaks heartbeats

my hands
become
her strings.

In the Break

William and Minnie
(known as Hotstuff and Dot),
Blues lovers at Doc's,
Lock in moist embrace,
Rehearse ancient rhythms:
The syncopation of lost crops,
Offbeat of muddy waters rising,
The percussion of survival years, useless.
They hold fast till the last
Musician's rest;
Push back, in cool, wet blackness.
This moment's smile will not soften winter fields,
But suits the break, j'es fine.

dancing with anger

that fool sent me a book
on how to manage my anger
how to keep all my rage
from ruining his groove
he said, I was thinking about you
and saw this in a bookstore
all innocent and sweet
like I'm doing this for us

but there is no us
and never could be
because I am an angry black woman
aka
sapphire
pirate jenny
erzulie dantor

and this poem/rant was prompted
by a confluence of events but I could
write another on any given day
because I am an angry black woman
and that's what we do

• • •

last week an elder bragged
about his olympian daughter
I asked what event
and he said she's a sprinter
then quipped
you know black women
always running one or the other
their legs or their mouths

and I wondered why he thought
it was ok to say that to me
to us
two black women with phds
both over thirty whom he
nevertheless referred to as
girls

what makes that shit funny and
what makes me wrong for being pissed off

when a brother gets angry about being pulled
over for driving while black
no one tells him that he needs to
manage his anger
no one buys him a book
or holds it against him
for hating all cops
every brother has the right
to be angry at
the man
but my man thinks I'm
dysfunctional
because I'm angry about my own oppression
and I don't hate brothers

• • •

(though sometimes they get on my nerves)
but I sure as hell don't feel like smiling
when I'm hissed at in the street and men
I don't know fondle every part of my being
with their liplicking cuntcursing tongues

and I don't feel like giving a hug
to the brother on tv
arrested tonight for forcing two teenage girls
to whore for him out in Queens
he beat and raped them himself in
between forcing the thirteen-year-olds to
service fifteen men per night
(rev dr dyson says shame on ya heh heh)
I guess pimpin works better as a metaphor

and I don't feel like laughing when I pick up usa
today and somewhere far from the front page
there's a story about a brother who stabbed
his neurosurgeon wife "several dozen times"
before hurling himself out a ten-storey window
and hitting the pavement soaked in her blood

what I need is a book
that will show me how to
keep my girlfriend safe from the ex
who called her this weekend
and threatened to take her life
the cops say there's nothing they can do
and she doesn't even want to file a report
because that would just make him ANGRY

. . .

maybe HE needs a book
even more than I do
because *I* sure as hell didn't set things up this way
and yes I am angry
but that rage keeps me from choking
on the tip of my own tongue
because my silence won't protect me
and I don't know who will

I'm a black woman in a world
that despises my femaleness
and patronizes my youth
and exoticizes my appearance
yet still expects me to SMILE
and be there for my man when he gets
passed over for promotion or
dropped from the team or
fired from a low-paying job
cause what do *I* know about oppression?

and seems everywhere I look
sisters are taking it lying down or
on the way back up a pole
even the ones who call themselves womanists
say you've got to let a man be a man
and the sisters who dared to speak the truth
are obsolete or
dead of cancer or
so far from the mic I can't hear
what they're whispering

• • •

and I'm tired of watching the same old scene
(a film classic, fully restored, now on dvd!)
nothing but a man my ass
that fool knocked abbey down and
she was carrying his child and
he never said sorry and
she never made him try and
in the end she took him back and
he decided to point his anger
where it actually belonged
(at The Man)
and nobody blamed him
for hating crackers or
for plotting revolution or
for trying to make the world
a better place for his unborn child

but *I* have anger issues
father issues
low self-esteem
I'm a borderline manhating lesbian
out to castrate what balls men have left
my tongue clips like a razor
my legs open and close like shears
my arms slide around their necks like a noose
and I leave them swinging in the breeze
black woman/black widow
anansi ain't got nothin on me

. . .

I am an angry black woman
a menace to straight brothers everywhere
but I am here to tell you that
I don't need a good book
or a good fuck
or some armchair psychologizing
from a man who can't hold that same mirror
up to himself

and yes I do eat sleep rant write live and
dance with anger
and if you don't like it
shame on ya
my life
and the lives of the women I love
are worth more than your
manly pride

and I wonder what might happen
if the things that make me angry
made you angry too

CHRISTOPHER GILBERT

She

for Carolyn Grace

When she sits at the kitchen table
while she talks her hands are a balance
in the air faithful at the level of
her words; she is careful what she says.
The morning sun through the window strikes
her skin, shows how the faint lines in her
palms will come to deepen like corduroy
cloth to fit the weather of her age.
Still a young woman, she has to work
the graveyard shift; sleeps what is left,
then wakes to get the kids to school.
It must be morning when she dreams.
Peering into her coffee's surface,
she looks back from its depth, her hands
caught holding an implement, a fossil of
her life: Alabama born, feelings
huddled north, these steel cities this cold month,
her dark soul twisting into fingers
whose motion at this brown angle
is the slow fall flight of leaves through time.
And she rises with the gesture, and
the oil in her hands is necessity's
sweat: each hand on the tabletop
a work cloth rubbing the other fine
sculptured one.

A Good Showing

This wasn't no wear all black funeral. Uncle Al showed up in a royal
blue suit with matching royal blue, pointed toe, snakeskin Stacy
Adams. Cousin William wore royal, too. But with blue-and-white
wingtips and a bit more gold around his neck. Most of the men were
content to wear traditional blacks and blues, leaving color to the
women. Mama wore her Christmas suit, the color of lemon crème,
once assured by her sisters that no one would remember it from the
holiday four months earlier. I wore a houndstooth suit, and over that
a Persian lamb mink collar coat Aunt Jean had found for me at the
Goodwill. Mama did my makeup and said I looked like a movie star.
We all looked good—filling up the pews of the church. Mama was
glad a lot of people showed up to grandma's funeral. Lena Pearl
Hollins wasn't one for making friends too kindly, or for keeping
them close, either. But that day everyone made a good showing.

The sun did not shine, but at least it did not rain. I didn't cry but
once, when cousin Jamil sang, "Goin' up Yonder," his fourteen-
year-old falsetto sounding angel pure and sweet. And then I felt my
heart fall softly when the funeral home man pulled the light blue
shroud off the sky grey casket, folded it quick and neat, and placed
it over grandma's white-gloved hands. He closed the heavy lid. You
almost could not hear the click.

Tradition/Abstraction

after Gilberto Gil

I met this girl who was visiting Atlanta. She looked
So sweet. She went around with this tough girl,
This very smart girl. So tough, she walked alone
At night. So smart, no one ever bothered her.

She walked with a wide gait and always looked people in the eye.
Singing sometimes. Sometimes just thinking. I met this girl
In Atlanta who looked sweet. She was visiting. This was when
Tribe was still together, before Tupac and Biggie got killed.

This was when we still protested Freaknik. Sometimes singing.
I met this girl in Atlanta at a party in a church on the corner
Of JP Brawley before the library "Club Woody." "Club Woody"
Because you could meet people there.

Sometimes in the stacks. Sometimes in the carrels.
Everyone else, that is, not me. This was right after
They beat the students on MLK. This was right when
I started to get jaded. Jaded, but still I believed

This girl's sweet way, visiting Atlanta. Her way was so sweet,
It made her friend sweet. Her friend who was so tough and so smart,
Walking down any street alone at night, looking them in the eye.
Singing. Or just thinking. Everyone else, that is. Everyone else.

. . .

Sometimes, visiting Atlanta, I met this girl. Her friend,
She walked, just singing. Think so smart. Night right sweet.
Just one them. This was no bother, believe. Every eye, that is,
Not alone. Looking street in the way. Girl. Some tough else.

sky in west memphis

on this night
we swat mosquitoes
eat falling stars
before they reach the earth
your love is silver
caught in my throat

Photo of My Mother

My mama never danced at the card parties
just swayed and snapped her fingers
to Sam Cooke's groove. She was a sexy woman
then, red hair and lips
fingernails, too.
In a photo I found last week, she stares
at me: legs crossed, high heels
mini-skirt, beer and cigarette.
A year before my birth
she is not yet thirty.
Three kids at home, her man in plain view.
She leans against a paneled wall
beside her a loudness looms like magnolia.
It is Mississippi in her eyes—
still Mr. Charles' daughter
the one who puts her foot in some greens
drinks coffee from saucers.

Good Times

Mami can't stand *Good Times*.
Every time the theme song comes on,
bursting through the RCA, she runs from the kitchen
and cranks the rickety dial, 2-3-5-4,
till it stops on Carol Brady or Shirley Jones.

Though God says we're not supposed to hate anything,
I know Mami hates that show. She gets really nervous
when J.J.'s father gets angry at something stupid J.J. does.
I think she can't take it when Mrs. Evans makes a fist, yells out something
that rhymes with *sam*, a word I'm not even *supposed* to know.

Even if Mami doesn't like Mrs. Evans,
I do. She has my mother's waist,
and her name is like the sun, toast-warm like postcards
from cousins on coastlines
I will never meet.

My mother makes a face every time
J.J. lets out his *dyn-o-mite!* a splinter getting under her skin,
her eyes on my brother, a baby crying on the floor.
No matter how much rice and beans she makes
him eat, he's still skinny as a beanpole.

. . .

She whispers at the TV set about those way-back-then days,
when boys with thin mustaches loved her.
"*Ay, look at that Thelma—if only I still had that Coca-Cola bottle.*"
I ask about the empty ones sitting all sticky under the sink,
but she gets up and changes the channel.

My brother and sister and me would get into a lot of trouble
if we slammed doors like they do in the Evans' house.
And so what if we don't have a Black Jesus to pray for our salvation—
my grandmother swears that, if we're good,
la Virgencita del Cobre might save us.

We don't have really tall smoky buildings to look out at.
Only a city of pecan trees watch. We crack their nuts,
let the shells get lost in the leaves wrestling around our feet.
While we play outside the trailer's kitchen window,
Mami mixes red Kool-Aid in a plastic pitcher.

What if the whole time she's dreaming of ice-cold coconuts,
green and sweaty in her palms?

My Father Stands at the Mississippi River Bridge

Maybe the cold brought you
back, the snow clumped like fur

on your neck, or the radiance of ice
clinging to rocks along the narrow river.

Did you hear the steel grates creak,
the harsh wind cracking on the beams?

Whoever turned you away
from your private sorrow, it wasn't

your wife. She is on a train
watching the frozen white fields fly

backwards in the window, moving
towards you.

Did the water cramp
and roar from below? Were you thinking

of declarations: yes, no, never,
always, this is the last time.

Were you so sure there was nothing
worse than grief? You will ache

. . .

when your first child breaks from the birth
canal coiled in her mother's cord.

You will sit with your father
drinking bourbon by the woodstove.

His house will flame so bright after nightfall,
the rooster will crow.

Whatever made you choose to live
through this trouble, will place you

in desert cities. You will be lost
in another tongue by a salt-crusted sea.

You will never know the future,
so you can bear to go forward.

Someplace below the Mason Dixon

i wanna move

to a place where we can walk hand in hand between rows of watermelons and yellow
cucumber flowers   sell sunflowers and green apples   on the corner or
from the frontporch
with red hand-painted signs   while drinking lemonade sweettea   and
eating hot caramel cake

i wanna drive fast

down dirt roads with no names   laughin' and lookin' in the rear view
mirror just in time to see
dust fly into the sky

i wanna go

to a people place where   tractors wait   for roosters and roosters wait
for the sun
where   people ride rusty bicycles   and trees dance with sunsets
where
where creamy hot buttered grits are for eating   not throwin' on some
cheatin' man
where neighbors come in without knockin'   i am not afraid
because you lie naked nexttome in a brass bed
under
two patchwork quilts

. . .

i need to retreat

to a space so w i d e   open   there is no place to hide   when
    things go wrong except
within your arms

someplace where we   can collect untamed horses   and never stop
    ridin'

i need to go

where   revolution is the moon serenadin' the sky

i wanna move deep south with you
wannamovedeepsouthwithyou

Girls Named Peaches

remind me of bubble gum, Mary Janes
and double-dutch interrupted
by their mama hollering from the front porch
PEEE-*chez*, go down to the store and pick me up some J&B.

make me wish I was my brother's girlfriend
as they sit tongue-tied in the den,
his hands stroking the creamy skin swelling
out of her too tight, unbuttoned blouse,
whispering: Come on, Peaches.

let me know what Nina is talking about
she sang "Mississippi Goddamn" right
as Rosa was fixing to take her seat,
what my mama screamed after
two white boys spit at her from their car:
Who do you think you is gal?
My name is Peaches.

keep me laughing when they tell me it's their given name,
saccharine on the tongue, juicy with the promise
of an ass swinging in denim, too ripe
as ready to be plucked as Janie under a pear blossom.

put me in mind of Georgia license plates,
twelve different streets with the same name,
the flesh of Auntie Renee's cobbler, a dark bruise
on a young woman's smiling face,
the promise of love's bitter sweetness spoiled.

Ms. Gladys Debro

my great aunt
got squash gourds
for titties

went to Atlantic City monthly
came back with ashtrays
made into ornate vaginas

tossed a head of Jheri curls
sipped molasses black coffee
with rum

told me
menstruation
was regal

said I was a southern gal
had to keep my shit tight
for a real man

had no shame ever
no babies
just her knickknacks

. . .

but I swear

in that old wedding picture
her thigh inflamed
in garnet nylons

she look
fertile
as all hell

cleaning graves in calvert

for Papa Johnny Hodge, my Great-Great-Grandfather

under a crying elder willow
we met. the 107 degree shade
bearing thirsty earth
from which i sprang.

a safehouse next door to
a tinderbox church.

sanctuary from hot

lone star nights.
though your face is hidden
i feel you
in the folds of mama's hands.

in my blood
i hear you. calling
beyond tired summer
crops to bring us here.

ritual precedes emancipation
(we were the last to know).
scrubbing dirt from your headstone.
gathering scattered branches.

Prevalence of Ritual

these women
these salteaters
from bearden's prevalence of ritual
purl untucked sheets left over from baptism
reset a paraffin lamp recessed in lichen
a perched daguerreotype atop
a scarred chifforobe
clutches an unknown girl standing beside
trumpeter swans
the inscription reads lucinda 1879 kilmarnock
its wings appear to cloak her hairline forming a muted halo
but it's only the birthing caul   she came seeing   an already
the camera angles her brand
she's wearing a loose burnoose shawl
from potato sacks
crushed glass beneath her left foot
shines nacre from her shore
borrowed from turtle island
on the back of the frameless capture
a scrawl   "somma dem bones is mine"

leaving mississippi

m i
crook a letter crook a letter i
crook a letter crook a letter i
humpback humpback i
your back curves like a scythe
and like a scythe on long grass your tongue
tames the past.
mississippi is your longest word:
single word story full of sibilant hesitations,
snaky swampy word you escaped
and reviled, and took with you
in your pots, on your tongue, beneath your fingernails.
a word twined you to the ones you left behind
and did not leave. word
full of repetitions, letters crooked
and hunchbacked. like you, great-grandmother,
miss arana johnson,
osteoporotic and bent when they brought you
to chicago.

you taught me how to count the "esses"
and the "pees" for my spelling bee at school,
said i didn't need to bother my head
about nothing more than the three r's.
but once i saw you,
gran arana, force your bent back straight—
you towered six feet tall,
hesitated, then eased back
to your cane.

A History of Beauty

Mother told me I'm from a line
of technicolor women with mountains

of breasts and wide laps that held nursing children
or steel bowls filled with June peas. With words,

they were acrobats. Tongues colliding
with a firmness as flexible and specific

as Ma Rainey lyrics, matching memories of bent backs,
third-grade geography books, midnight riders,

unplanned births, but there is something more.
Like nightingales, their sounds of love and loss

echo in kitchens, bouncing off hot-plate-brewed
coffee and two-day-old biscuits sopping up Karo

syrup. In their songs they remember the feeling
of that first kiss as they followed their men

to northern cities; men who bit their tongues,
ate dirt, dust and their pride. Worked anywhere.

These women knew only a blues could mask
the painful smell of faces stuck to the goggles

• • •

their men wore in steel factories. Now, they have
no time for beauty, theirs left in wind whispering

through bulrush, the teeming taste of scuppernong
grapes, the anticipation of a ham dotted with a patchwork

of cloves spinning on a spit and hints of honey-
suckle buried freely in the folds of their flesh.

A Twice Named Family

I come
from a family
that twice names

its own.
One name
for the world.

One name
for home.
Lydi, Joely, Door,

Bud, Bobby, Bea,
Puddin, Cluster, Lindy,
Money, Duddy, Vess.

Yes,
we are
a two-named family

cause somebody
way back knew
you needed a name

to cook chitlins in.
A name
to put your feet up in.

• • •

A name
that couldn't be
fired.

A name
that couldn't be
denied a loan.

A name
that couldn't be
asked

to go
through anyone's
back door.

Somebody way back
knew we needed names
to be loved in.

Juke Joint Josephine

She is blacker than a bruised big toenail,
Tough, scaly, defiant as the blues.
A champagne glass on her gold tooth
Matches champagne-colored shoes.

She laughs. Says my boat can't possibly
Be big enough to plow through her wet sea.
I say, "Drowning? Between hips like those?
Don't think you're scaring me."

Says she's seen my kind and knows me well:
Seditty. Too stiff to get down.
Demands to know why I'm here again
On her broke-down side of town.

It's my fascination with full, round breasts
And the women who carry them proud,
Sweet perfume on sweaty necks,
Blue Bland blaring loud.

I'm Mississippi, born and bred,
With a big city education,
Know Ovid, Chaucer, Goethe, Keats
Plus some old Greek conjugations.

But I wants a woman who will send me on
Her most intimate feminine errands
And love me till I start to drop
The *g*'s off all my gerunds.

girl meets girl

girl i knows you something else this i cannot lie
say girl i knows you something else this i cannot lie
prayed to god for true love and he stuck eve in my eye

now what am i to do with this husband of mine?
say what am i to do with this husband of mine?
seems his sun only shines when my back is to the ground

i'm gonna wrap this little man up send him on his way
say i'm gonna wrap this little man up send him on his way
and pray a good woman finds him before judgment day

because girl i knows you something else this i cannot lie
and loving you makes me so damn happy i aint even gonna try

martha will go looking for jesse again

at sunrise
after their daughter's ghost
climbs out of bed
& saunters to the bathroom
across the hall
disturbing the water bugs
fast asleep beneath the floorboards.

no one will be there to smooth a warm hand
over the chill bumps
rising like corn muffins on martha's arms
nor brush away the wet ribbons
lining her face in fear
though it has been eight years
since an ice cream truck
sent belinda flying off her bicycle
& onto a neighbor's yard
trampling prize-winning sunflowers
& breaking the noses of daffodils.

. . .

but when martha leaves her house
hoping to find jesse
behind the walls of his father's jazz club
passed out like a saxophone
slung over a piano
a woman named ella will be standing at the door
ready to tell martha
she saw her husband shoot himself
then leave his body for a weepy little girl
who claimed she was too scared
to ride to heaven
on anything with wheels.

Dinah

And Dinah the daughter of Leah,
which she bare unto Jacob, went out
to see the daughters of the land.
— Genesis 34:1

I grew up watching them cut their eyes,
grit their teeth at each other.
My aunt entering a room
stiffened my mother. They warred
years over that old man
asleep in the back room—
my father, spent.

Their weapons: sons
they pushed from their bodies.
My mother bore six,
prayed with each *Now*
he will not hate me. He
will not wipe himself
with the sheet, leave
my bed without looking
back. Tonight,
when he comes he will
not picture my sister.
I never played with girls,

• • •

only this army
of brothers they mustered
feeding my father female
bodies, other women snatched
into his bed, delivered
like sacrifices. They consumed
themselves, wasteful, greedy.

When I went
out into the city
that day I wanted to meet
women who looked
at each other,
whose bodies kept
their softness in
the presence of their sisters.
Instead, I met a man,
relearned
my family's definitions
for love, body, weapon.

Turn in by the Silver Queen
and Double Twisted Pine

The Definition of Place, 1963

after A. Van Jordan

place (plas) n. [<Blk. org. jook joint, *the spot*.] **1a)** bootleg house: there is a jukebox in the corner of this *place*, plays low-down dirty blues, kind of blues that sings about a man holding on till help come along and if don't no help come along he still holding on. kind of blues where if the world stopped rotating on its axis and fell into a corner pocket, everything be easy as long as he got a woman and a drank. **b)** building: this is a *place* where men in solid uniforms or Liberty overalls congregate for good times after wrestling with Mr. Charlie. **2a)** repose: as in *place* where iron ore strength can breathe easy, is a different nigger. the hornet's sting pacified by fifty-cent shots straight down the throat, and the burn is heaven. a second home that is organic. can't be swayed by governor's office or state mandate that propagates: separate but never equal. this *place* got its own beauty. **b)** situation: women search this *place* for thickheavy fingers on breasts, live by darkness in shotgun houses on cement stilts with three kids and no daddy, wait for someone who can deliver them from foot tub washing. there are rooms with squeaky box springs; air filled with yesterday's loving and today's possibility. where ain't nobody mad but folks that ain't gettin' none. **3)** structure: space or *place* devoted for specific purposes: to drink moonshine, play bid whist, fuck, and have got-damn good time. **4)** region: in the lower part of Alabama there is a city / a town / a *place* called Birmingham where Negroes refuse to curl up and die.

Collection Day

Saturday morning, Motown
forty-fives and thick seventy-eights
on the phonograph, window fans
turning light into our rooms,
we clean house to a spiral groove,
sorting through our dailiness—
washtubs of boiled white linens,
lima beans soaking, green as luck,
trash heaped out back for burning—
everything we can't keep,
make new with a thread of glue.

Beside the stove, a picture calendar
of the seasons, daily scripture,
compliments of Everlast Interment
Company, one day each month marked
in red—PREMIUM DUE—collection visit
from the insurance man, his black suits
worn to a shine. In our living room
he'll pull out photos of our tiny plot,
show us the slight eastward slope,
all the flowers in bloom now, how neat
the shrubs are trimmed, and *See here,*
the trees we planted are coming up fine.

• • •

We look out for him all day, listen
for the turn stop of wheels
and rocks crunching underfoot.
Mama leafs through the Bible
for our payment card—June 1969,
the month he'll stamp PAID
in bright green letters, putting us
one step closer to what we'll own,
something to last: patch of earth
view of sky.

A Far Cry

I make a wrong turn in the suburbs
and get lost in the backwoods of Tennessee
with nothing to protect my African body
but a Japanese car.

Trees night the sky. There's a man
driving behind me. I think he can tell by the nap
of my hair. I think he will follow me
into a driveway if I try to turn around.

How far is Alabama?
Which doorstep shall I dare
to darken? What makes them
tear our flesh sometimes?

A ghost of a woman stands roadside,
waving down cars. I follow her flashlight
to an old barn where some have gathered
for an unknown cause. Could be church

or a hanging but all I trust
is the strange out here, and this
blank-faced beacon is strange
as a bush on fire. So I put on

. . .

my ancestors' armor. A smile,
a shuffle, a voice I lace with *please*
and a twang. Anything to remind them
of the ones who know how to bow their heads.

Only then do I heel-toe through the mud
to the barn, where three white men
wait in the doorway. Wait watching me, a small,
brown woman. A stranger, crossing their land.

Letter from Cuba

It takes two full days away before I stop worrying about my work.
On the third day, I go back to stops on the tour from the day before; and by
the end of the fourth day, whether I see more sights no longer matters.
After a week, I think I could leave my life.

I have been here longer than I can say.
There are moments I am in Goldsboro or Mobile or Savannah, and it is the
time we are children and the
weather hot, and the people mostly our family, and the air is fragrant
with flowers, mud stink, and kerosene, and there are crops to be cut.

My heart is nearly breaking.
One afternoon, I sat in the white sand and looked across the Atlantic.
I thought how long ago some of us ended up here and some of us ended up
there.
Restlessness still washes me over in waves.

Kind and handsome men come up to me to practice their English, they want
to sell me cigars and
rum, a cheaper room, a meal at a cousin's paladar, a woman,
themselves.
No, no, I say. I want you to tell me the stories.
We walk or we sit down and eat, and I listen, asking, I'd like please to practice
my Spanish.
When you see me again, my brother, my sister, I will be calmer.

. . .

The Yoruba priest tossed cowrie shells several times at my feet, telling me to make offerings to
    hold on to my money, to be protected from accidents, for me to be married.
He told me I could change, if I wanted.
He didn't know what I wanted him to know about me.
And I was surprised to learn what I wanted.

One day, walking the center of Havana, I tripped and fell to my knees.
I'd been looking up at crumbling buildings, I was listening to music coming from someone's
    open windows, and I was trying to place a voice.
Everyone moved toward me with concern.
I'm fine, I kept saying in English, thank you.
It's true what they say: there is beautiful music here, and it is everywhere.

There is music some places in the world that makes me wish.
Instead of settling down, I could have wandered.
I could have loved some others; I could have loved much more.
I could have lived other lives.

Where you from, Martinique? Bahamas? Americano? You like Tupac?
I'm not sure I know the America they ask me about.
I tell them I listen to the blues. I tell them I listen to opera.
Sometimes, on the way home from work, I hear salsa.

The poet who read only in Spanish made me close my eyes.
I was falling and falling into a voice.
Not knowing her language, I finally heard the poems.
And when it was my turn, mi hermana, mi hermano, waters swelled deep within me,
    and I spoke back.

Farm Bureau Advisor

They suggested that the man who taught them
not to choke fields with tight turns of growing
but to sometimes let them breathe as deeply
as uncorseted girls, the one black man
they ever knew the government to trust
with a job and a salary, the man
who lectured at the University
when few of them read further than their names
across a ledger, yes, they suggested
that Thornton's father must have forgotten
his place when he bought that new Ford model
and drove past town onto their country roads,
and they warned him: *A horse and cart will do
just fine next time you come around these parts.*

Eddie Priest's Barbershop & Notary

Closed Mondays

is music   is men
off early from work   is waiting
for the chance at the chair
while the eagle claws holes
in your pockets   keeping
time   by the turning
of rusty fans   steel flowers with
cold breezes   is having nothing
better to do   than guess at the years
of hair   matted beneath the soiled caps
of drunks   the pain of running
a fisted comb through stubborn
knots   is the dark dirty low
down blues   the tender heads
of sons fresh from cornrows   all
wonder at losing   half their height
is a mother gathering hair   for good
luck   for a soft wig   is the round
difficulty of ears   the peach
faced boys asking Eddie
to cut in parts and arrows
wanting to have their names read
for just a few days   and among thin
jazz   is the quick brush of a done
head   the black flood around
your feet   grandfathers
stopping their games of ivory
dominoes   just before they reach the bone

yard   is winking widowers announcing
cut it clean off   *I'm through courting*
and hair only gets in the way   is the final
spin of the chair   a reflection of
a reflection   that sting of wintergreen
tonic   on the neck of a sleeping snow
haired man   when you realize it is
your turn   you are next

what if we'd had a bullet

what if we'd had a bullet
for the forehead of every bigot

what if we had castrated the real rapists,
hacked away their savage genitals
with razors, knives, and pruning shears

what if we had tapped their phones
maligned their gods
slammed their children against concrete walls
with fire hoses and murderous intent

if we had become expert
in the ways of retribution
who might we be today

have we dreamed the wrong dream

should we have learned to flay the skin
to gouge out eyes
to dance and grin and howl like fiends
as a man slowly roasts alive

should we have closed our eyes
not in prayer
but creative contemplation

. . .

surely we too could have found uses for the mundane—
the broken stick of a toilet plunger
a length of chain coiled in the back of a truck

properly harnessed
our collective imaginations
might otherwise have economized
41 bullets

but we have dreamed another dream
and I must admit that sometimes I wonder
what I am doing
here

what my life is worth
here

but I don't know where else to go
I confess to being terrified
of back roads in Texas
small towns in Oklahoma
and the police force of every major U.S. city

five year old girls are being raped in the Congo
and teenage girls are turning tricks on my block
and what stops me from ripping out some brothers' tongues
is the hope that just once they will call me
a woman

I need my own tongue
to ask these hard questions

if Malcolm had lived
to father his four daughters
would Betty be alive today

. . .

will rappers who got shot
loom larger in our memory
than true visionaries like
Audre and June

what if
after all
Jimmy was right
and there is no cure
for this pathology

will we speed the erasure
of entire generations

will nostalgia numb the pain
of living only to acquire

what I need is a place
somewhere on this planet
where I can transplant my sapling dreams
for too long they have lain
uprooted on the concrete
exposed
unnourished
in peril
in need

but if Coretta could forgive him
his indiscretions
and Du Bois had the courage
to spurn INS
then there must be at least some hope
for a young black woman
who wants a new homeland
and needs to be free

Charleston Inferno

Had the tattlers not tattled,
even babies

would've been pinned under flames,
white skin dancing apart to the jig,

Sins of the father
make this right.

But the tattlers did tattle
and Strom's kind

had a line.

Vesey knew:
spare an orphan or faithful Negroes,

their tongues and dicks are bound
to whittle vendettas.

They tried him.
I've tried him, too.

His testament, the slipped halo
round his throat.

Haiku 12005

Birmingham sun sits
On Sixteenth Street, witnessing
Slaughtered sunflowers.

Crum Road, Lyons, Mississippi

Myths start like this. Mother said not to forget the red rocks. How they crumbled with weight. How each step turned your head no matter how old you were it was always left foot, right foot, turn to see who followed. At best you were alone and each step seemed a leap closer to where you were going. No man-hands grabbing for female child. Father says nightriders still wait behind the pear trees. They know the children won't walk off the patch of grass and house. Sometimes, they leave hungry kittens, full bags of cotton. Sometimes, they pick fruit and leave it cored on the branch. Grandmother says snakes sneak out of cotton fields to breathe in our flesh. Vinnie and I climbed poplar trees to see for sure what lies on the road. We picked locust shells and tossed them out for bait. They crunched when cars rolled by. Leah asks if it's all true: If men raped little girls in the field; if snakes coil at the base of new stalks. Uncle Floyd says *ain't nothing out there but dirt roads leading to other dirt roads*. I'm inclined to believe him any other time. Aunt Gladys says a crocodile lives in the swamp by Crum Road. Says he floats with eyes open, skimming, waiting for something to slip into his path. The new blacktop won't stop him, she says. Yes. It's true.

Ode to the Triays of Amelia

I will die on Amelia,
the Isle of May.
It will be on a Wednesday
to give all my kinfolks enough time
to fly home from everywhere
for a Saturday funeral.

The kids will argue
about cremating me
then they'll remember I
told them there is no room
on the Black Catholic side
of Bosque Bello cemetery
which means "beautiful forest"
where the backdoor Triays
are buried, sons and daughters
of Spaniards and ex-slaves.

They will finally cremate me
and scatter my ashes
all over Old Town,
once entirely owned by
my Free Mulatto Triay grandfathers
who built the seawall on top of
Seminole bones and
who birthed the shrimping industry,
even though the Greeks and Italians
got all the credit.

. . .

They will scatter me some more
over what developers left unruined
of American Beach,
that we used to call
"the Black Beach" where
they made us go because they
didn't think we were American,
but where we were glad to go
because A. L. Lewis
made it our own.

Then they will scatter me
on "Amelia Island Plantation"
the rich white folks resort
built by developers
on the tombstones and homesites
of a desecrated Gullah-Geechee village.

I will not let them forget
"Historic Downtown Fernandina"
where they will rub some of my ashes
over the word "Traeye"
on the first British census
to anglicize my name.

Finally, they will scatter me
on the corner of Estrada Street
which means "to stride"
and Ladies Street
which was "Calle de las Damas"
where African and Mulatta whores
serviced the seafaring men and
offered low-rate placage
to nearby conquistadores.

• • •

And then, in due time, my ashes
will rise up in stride
quick-like into a storm
that will blow over
all of Amelia
and claim her once again as mine.

The Triays of Amelia Island, a Florida barrier island, are the African American
descendants of the slaveholding Triays of St. Augustine, one of the Spanish
(Menorcan) families who founded the city. Slave masters purchased land there for
their free mulatto offspring. Amelia shares a history similar to those of Hilton Head,
St. Helena's, and other U.S. barrier islands. Fernandina Beach is Amelia's main city.

Huddle House

You can tell they are lovers—
his perpetual frown
outshining her pink sweater,
the shoes to match

parked between his feet.
They find comfort in grease,
draining bacon across lips,
raking forks through the butter

swimming grits.
On a segregated jukebox,
Stevie Nicks wails,
Will you ever win?

over the sizzle & pop of the grill,
the tambourine rattle
of plates & silverware.
When the check is settled,

the couple leaves room
for other diners,
sour face & loud shoes
slow-stepping into a Kentucky

Sunday morning. The leftovers
grow cold.

BRANDON D. JOHNSON

At Junie's

her heels click like a .38's cylinders.
every smoke-dry eye in Junie's rolls her way, remembering
it's been three weeks since Cleatha left a man face down in here.
Bobby Bland gargles lament like a warning from the jukebox.

almost tall as a soda machine, dark as a pair of shades
she acts like nobody is paying attention to her long legs
thighs thick as cold molasses, eyes the color of cattails
and that white streak slashing through pinky-length hair.

seen men fight for anything or nothing cause of her.
seen women lick their lips, hear them wonder out loud
what it'd be like to have everybody in sight line wanting
a piece of you just for breathing so sexy.

wannabe players strut past, hands brushing crotches.
drawn to danger like bugs to Venus flytraps
they leer, imagine her paying their small issues mind,
as if her gripping a club was a practiced caress.

she walks to the bar sure as an 18-wheeler.
taller than anyone on the rail, she straddles a stool
without stepping up, doesn't look to either side.
Junie doesn't ask, just pushes a short dark

. . .

iceless glass in front of her, steps back into a shadow
and polishes a coffee cup as if gleaming porcelain mattered
to the next drunk patron fiending for the bottom of the pot.
Clagett ducks a door's arch, his upturned lips passing for a smile.

he's a mauled throwback to times when men were
all the rough clichés, lived up to them like jobs,
when women, accepting the situation,
cleaved without drama or fuss.

but after her man Hollowpoint painted Junie's parking lot
with himself and she'd left Melvin Peeples thinking
the Lord had thumped his head in for being worthless,
Cleatha found no reason to make any man think she cared for him.

so Clagett burrows into the end of the bar, swings an eye
her way and grins as if she were a pork chop smothered
in onions and a foot of grease. when she knocks one back to her tonsils,
bores the shot glass into the bar's wood, slurs to Junie *do ya job, baby,*
it's not clear whether she sees Clagett, or cares to.

he's concerned when that smile melts from his face
and he shouts for a setup. it appears he'll need to catch up
before he's going to be noticed by Cleatha, begins drowning
his tongue in whiskey as if it were already on fire.

right now, the joint is quiet, witnesses steal looks
at them like they were doing a gangland meet and greet.
voices stay low, the loudest sound being glass slamming
wood, and a small hoot each time a shot hits the spot.

Clagett's bald head shines under the lights. sweat sets
up top waiting for a hand swipe or a ride to the floor.
his eyes are dark as crab apples and the cloth
near his pits is doing overtime to hold his wetness in.

•   •   •

meanwhile, Cleatha throws three more down, an actual giggle
in her eyes. Junie needs track shoes. they're going to
kill *him* before they stop this face-off.

after her tenth, Cleatha turns her chin toward the big man
sees the rows of empty glasses Junie sweeps onto a tray get replaced
with more of the *water of life.* she looks impressed.
Clagett lifts one a little higher as if saluting a worthy adversary.

each rolls one down their throats in unison
slides another down the bar to click in front of Junie
pays no attention to the admiring crowd now feeling
safe to show they were watching

Cleatha ain't grinned since before February '65, but something
like that came across her face after a time. not sure
if it was the alcohol or the duel cooling her nerves, but
Clagett slides up to her, whispers a thing, and *real* smiles

flutter off their faces like butterflies from a field of flowers,
couldn't hear anything but body language saying too much to repeat.
that's when the air heats, starts burning like bread in a toaster.
seems elsewhere, last nerves are being trampled like a motel rug.

two men in the back of the club stop whispering.
cards fly to the ceiling, fall quick as the bad words
rolling off their tongues. booze sprays folks like skunk piss.
a quick fist lands square, ends a fight at the beginning.

Cleatha drops the bills for the next round and Clagett
don't appear to be bothered that a woman covers him.
whiskey flows long after the twelfth shot burns a grimace
to their lips, but no one pays them much mind now.

. . .

Sally slides up to a chick with her arm round Beetle
her razor's flash makes the woman *feel* cut. sequined skirt switches
out the door saying *child, I got work in the morning*
but we all know it's *Friday* night.

Joe Jones hooks a palm at a witty woman's ducking face, and loud
as firecrackers, he gets the jaw of the brother next to her.
folks watch steel-bred arms pimp toward Jones, him looking to
divine a solution for long life from the mug of sediment Junie sells.

some smart-ass plays Marvin's "After the Dance" to smooth the mood.
only because it lights flames in memory's boilers,
does anyone pause a breath. Clagett swivels on his stool, scans faces,
his eyes lighthouse lanterns warning ships of the ocean's teeth.

the message is received like radio, folks pick up coats
get checks and check that tips aren't too high.
sharp blue nails arc a bicep.
she whispers a smile into his ear, a gleam into his good right eye.

the last person in Junie's holds the door open for the couple
walks in the opposite direction toward the corner, looks over
his shoulder just as Clagett wraps an arm around Cleatha's narrow
waist and she plants her lips on the cheek with no scars.

Scintillating stars

Scintillating stars
against midnight-black expanse
cold Virginia nights

April's black canvas

April's black canvas
sprinkled with white stars gleaming
Virginia night sky

Harlem Cats

(Vintage 1940s)

Once, walking
down Seventh Avenue,
I saw two young men,
real cool
briskly dip-
walking,
One North,
One South
they recognized
each other,
without breaking
the dip-walk
clipped words
in the wind
as they passed
said it all,
Man
Yeah
Dig
Later
Spikey's

Barking

Now it's twilight, I walk
the boundaries of the farmstead,
caught in snowflakes.
A sudden bark echoes and echoes again
in the distance. And still,
groping toward that voice,
I come to a splintered barn
that leans beside a dried pond.
This is where the hacked-down trees
lie among ferns, leafless
and slender like beanpoles.
So I stop here, then see the ruins
of the stable. I close my eyes.
This reminds me of my grandfather
who worked the farm from dawn to dusk;
and it was always summer.
At the edge of the starlit woods
and standing still like a statue,
I think: even now, I cannot walk
from this farm of my dream.

in a place where

crape myrtle hangs
brushes the ground
japanese beetles ride each other's back
the leaf eaten away beneath them
hills and mountains carve out the sky
random pieces in a rag quilt
queen anne's lace, ragweed
sweetpeas and joe-pye weed
choke the roadsides
and there are no signs stating

wildflowers do not pick

in a place where
crows big as cats
feed in fields dotted with wagon-wheel hay bales
cattle, flies sipping from their eyes
seek shade from trees along the fence line
in a place where
you drink a breath and hay
manure, magnolia and wild primroses
ride the intake of air
a dirt road swallowed by pines
smoke rises above silver maples
the smell of hog-killing hangs in the air

• • •

heavy shoes crunch gravel
down and up an incline
to the trailer
offset by trash, circled by weeds
on a mattress in the front yard
crumpled and headless
a black man burns

July 25, 1997; G. P. Johnson
was burned alive and decapitated
in rural, Grayson County, Virginia,
in a place where
I, call home

Garden

I too have turned
to the yard

turning the yard
into

frustration of flowers
I have felt for

a knot in the soil
coaxing pulling at

bindweed roots
pulling gently so

they give
half inch by half inch

the vines wound
silently violent

round the necks
of black eyed

susans
Name each

•   •   •

flower and the yard
loses

ground becomes

brunnera bleeding
heart bearded

iris peony purple
coneflower lupine

lily
I enter

the garden
I enter hackles raised

One finger then two three four
sliding into the earth

It falls away from itself like
cake crumbs

If I lower my mouth to it
I can catch the grains

of dirt on my lips
sweep them

away
with my tongue

A man who wanted to tie me
to a tree once licked

. . .

raw sugar from
my open hand

a policeman he wanted me
to behave

like an animal
From yard to garden

misprision a prisoning
measure   of space

I hold up my hand and
drizzle strikes at

every target but my palm

I cannot be touched
by anything above me

O'Connor's South

I
I read a sign aloud that said
Open air fires unlawful before 4 p.m.
while driving through Emporia
with Princess and Til. We laughed until
someone said   *That's why you never see
crosses burning before evening*, half-smiling
as we made our way further South.

II
When we sped by—three brown women staring,
my right pointer aimed at a black-faced lawn jockey
decorating a sweaty white man's lawn—the man, out gardening,
snapped his neck to watch. At the stop sign not twenty feet
from his azaleas, I looked back, am sure I saw him
lean toward his 'artificial nigger' and whisper.

III
Ice cream seemed the only thing cool enough
to combat South Carolina's September swelter,
but the marquee at Dairy Dream didn't advertise
two scoops for the price of one or free sprinkles.
Suffering truth decay   it read—light reflecting
the Baptist steeple towering across the street—
Read your Bible. Get a treat.

. . .

IV
In hours, my grandfather would bury his mother
and wanted a bulb for her porchlight—left burning
for elderly guests paying respects
in the night. When he asked for 75 watts,
the man behind the counter gave him 40.
My grandfather pointed out the difference
but the man didn't budge, just asked   *Boy,*
what y'all need all that light for?

bliss: geophagy

Humming underwing, vast sky erupts from | dirt and gravel road. Our animal creeping returns | me, tamed, to land: every loss balanced. In the middle of | a wood, there is water table and a well, uncovered, drinking rain. | A lull, a rumble. My throat, elongated supple sponge | absorbs defiant syllables with soft resolve; | the earth bellows, rushing in

Bowing in the Church of Beauty

Hymns are swinging low
from a cassette boom box
pulsing between dusty bottles
of curl activator and ancient blow out kits
made new in the contemporary retro wave.

Worshippers return from Sunday service
to their respective houses of beauty
where baptized kinks become straight
and narrow as the good books decree.

Jet—Old Testament
Essence—New Testament
O—Queen Winfrey's Version

These sistas sing and shout
a joyful noise louder than the whirring
hair dryers blowing a hot freeze
over stylish bouffant crowns.

Got to look good for the week's worst
they say and *God don't like ugly.*
I know. Not wanting to be rude
my wild atheist hair bows at the sink's edge,
if not for salvation, at least congregation.

Awake

In a graveyard of bones,
the lovers lay on freshly cut grass,
sniffing the aroma of roses and red dirt.

She hadn't understood why he brought her here.
There were plenty of places they could have gone.
Life in the country is rife with dirt roads, clay paths
and dead ends, where classmates brag of lewd exploits
after Friday night football games. But Gerald said
he liked graveyards at night, the silent smell of flowers,
intensity of stars, the order of it all: mounds of dirt
in neat rows like his mother's garden in spring,
pale headstones reflecting the moon's reflected light.

He emerged from the yellow Camaro
pulling a tattered blue blanket from the backseat,
stood for a long minute eyeing the commune
of the dead, melancholy fascination consuming
his angular face.

He spread the blanket between two new graves,
and for several moments, they lay quietly
savoring the sweet sound of their breathing.

in my neighborhood just north of atlanta

hummers line the asphalt groves
wooly-tooth mammoths   trudge everything
pound toward the bp station to guzzle
at its pond   suck it dry

the villagers   once pale   now southern-fried
ride high on its back   shaded by versace
they buy the sun   plant concrete-seeds
water them with 10w40

breed money-greens from their favored land
fertilize with smog   their secret
overnight a crop   *paint still wet*   appears
they sell at market on same street;

around the corner   in the underbelly
men hold signs   *will work for food*   plant themselves
in their own dirt and sweat   ear to the ground
heed the pound of the mammoth.

Milledgeville Haibun

Beat. Beat. Beats beat here. The sound of the train on the Georgia road, the measured claps of the wheels at the gaps of the joints of the rails is the beat of the hammer on iron and anvil at the smithy, Sol's shop, shaping shoes for mules and horses; and the sizzle of red metal in water is the train's whistle, and all echoes resound and effuse, and the last word returns like watermelons here with summer heat, beat with a hammer, beat when he, a boy, broke into the garden at the county jail at night when the beat men were asleep because theirs were the sweetest, so bust one open, the dull thud just before the crack, and eat the heart and move on to the next; and he moved on to women and settled eventually on one and finally busted her with finality, thud before crack, and he measured time raising the sweetest watermelons for a time and time served he returned, a man, and he lay on the tracks of the Georgia road cradled by the rails. Heart stopped.

> Old railroad, abandoned—
> between crossties trees grow,
> a feral pig roots below branches.

Fifth Street Exit, Richmond

1
Leave the freeway at this point.
Drive off where a chain-link fence
separates the road from a patch of weeds
and forces you past a row of ancient houses dying
from the fever of progress. Hurry past.
Proceed with cautious speed down Fifth Street
to Main, beyond the place where death lurks, where
airy ghosts peer through the dust of floor-long
windows and scream with hollow voiceless mouths.

2
The phantom children are calling,
they are calling my name.
They are playing hide-and-seek
by yellow streetlight and
they cannot find me. I am busy
chasing fireflies.
The phantom children are calling,
calling my name.

3
I could go back if I wanted to.
I could join the dance again
bouncing my feet with theirs
on the sidewalk of uneven brick
as they jump   jump
and jump   Jim   Crow.

• • •

I could learn again to make
the swooping gesture
Cotton needs a-pickin' so-o-o bad
in rhythm with their song
(graceless newcomer from the North
but eager to be one with them).
Cotton needs a-pickin' so-o-o bad
I'm gonna pick all over this land.
I *could* do it again.
If I wanted to.

4
The clop-clop-clop of horses' hooves,
the clatter of wagon wheels on cobblestones
bring the street vendor to the shade
of our magnolias.

Above the horses' whinnying
his cindery voice, half-song, half-wail,
bellows, blasts across
the heavy air.

> *Get your fresh watermelon,*
> *Sweet melon, cold melon,*
> *Black-seeded juicy melon,*
> *Ripe melon sweet.*

Oh, the spicy redolence of summer!
Oh, the freshfruit glories of Southern
summertime!

> *Watermelon, sweet melon,*
> *Black-seeded fresh melon,*
> *Come buy your watermelon,*
> *Ripe melon sweet.*

. . .

5

Wil and Clarence and Dadie and Lew
played mumblety-peg by the curb, and Suzie
whimpered and put up her hair in balls
while Bubba chased me around the yard, and

Grampa died and Bubba cried
and knocked me down and gashed my head
and Dadie's father stitched my wound
and Sadie cut my hair that summer

and seasons came and long years went
and Richmond just kept coming back
and we were grown before we guessed
the wonder that those summers meant.

6

I wish I *could* go back
to the cool green shuttered dark
that hid us from the boisterous sun,

from the explosion of color and fragrance outside,
back into the cocoon,

back to the Concord grapes ripening
in the arbor where the swing hung still
patient   waiting   for the evening cool—

afternoon baths and starched white
eyelet dresses with blue sashes
and patent leather shoes:

    Richmond summers chocolate
    as childhood's toothsomest delights.

I wish I could.

. . .

7
Azalea petals fell for the last time
one spring and tried in vain
to fertilize this asphalt garden.
The bricks crumbled and were hauled away,
the green shutters fell to dust
and where Grandma's white-pillared porch
once welcomed Sunday callers
a chain-link fence went up to mark an exit
from Wherever, U.S.A., to Main Street, Richmond.

Leave the freeway at this point and don't,
oh, don't go back. Don't listen
to the children's hollow voices
chanting elegies to the whir
of wheels turning, turning.

Summer Night, McNasby's Pier, 1968

My sister walks me down
to the end of our street. The pier past
McNasby's Oyster House juts out
into the darkness, a finger pointing east.

We cross the broken shells carefully,
a jagged carpet, white and pearl,
the smoothest shards reflecting the full moon,

to sit at the pier's end, look out
at the dark still water, the last Chesapeake Bay
tour boat of the evening a floating house on fire,
a silent, moving blaze of yellow light.

Air rising between the pier's slits
is cool, cooler than the night, the rhythmic
clang of tackle against mast the perfect music

for calling sleep. So many questions I want to ask:
Why do the stars blink? Why are they
turned off at dawn? Why is our father distant?
Why did our mother die? *Hush*, she says,

Lean back. Side by side we lie staring up
at the black night, the bay an acrid perfume
in our noses, cool air more like a blanket

. . .

around my shoulders than the sheet I find myself
wrapped in by morning, night transformed to day,
not knowing when I'd drifted off to sleep, been lifted
up, brought across sharp edges, carried home.

duke

no job
sleeping in the backseat of a car
moving from town to town
that's how it starts
that's how it begins
here in louisiana
where the money
once was like oil
slick and black

now the dirt is dust
the hunting is gone
and the river doesn't answer
when you call

so what can i tell you about david duke
except that he knows these parts, these people
and the inside of their prayers
papers say he a racist but who ain't these days
colored ain't no different from the whites
in that regards . . .
i knew his daddy and both of them come from
small towns no bigger than this one
start right here with some of my best friends
beer drinking, blue jean wearing, dixie hummin
folks like myself

. . .

that's why i voted for him
i took him by his word
and his word was white folks need to
organize before colored folks do
you take a man by his word
and sometimes it's as good
as your own hand in your pocket

now you know what i do?
i pick politicians mostly by their wives
if she look like she's been cheated on
i can tell at them rallies and press conferences
any man cheat on his wife
will do anything to deny it
but you know if he lie to his wife
he just might be one of the boys
i don't mind that   that's politics
that's how the system works

i don't confess to messing with
any colored gals but i know a few
fellas who have
but it wasn't nothin
just a little fun on a friday night

like chasing those civil righters
those northern boys and jews

in the old days we had a lot of fun
and the colored kids the little ones
knew how to laugh, beg for money, shine
shoes, and dance

now if you put some of these grown-up boys
in a voting booth there's no telling
what they'll do

. . .

i need a job just as much as my wife
needs love
you know what i'm talking about?

the first time i heard david duke
speak i knew things were getting better
i'm tired of someone putting words in
the mouths of politicians

it's about time a white man speak the truth
if you don't want to hear the truth
then you don't know what the truth is

i love this country
this louisiana
this place where good food is just
waiting to be fixed
and the stars shine every night
like children when you give them sweets

don't let me ever catch the river running
the wrong way
i don't know what i do
what can a man believe in if things change?
david duke he's alright
he talks the way i talk
and this is louisiana
you a stranger if you don't know it

Of Course the Brochure Doesn't Mention Mrs. Abbott

Saint Simon's Island, Georgia

The people here say when a hurricane stretches
and reaches Category 3, sometimes

the ocean comes up to Ocean Boulevard, but
the fish do not

come to shop at the Gates of St. Simon's. Today
is Sunday morning and I'm biking along Lord Avenue.

How religious can I get without calling myself
to preach the gospel according to Luke. Everyone

speaks, this morning, to me, the happy brown stranger
in town wearing a tan fishing hat with hooks tucked
in

to the science of not catching, but at the same moment
catching, the Sunday slow morning ambience
like strained blue church window glass here in this town

where hurricanes can rearrange the cityscape in the fall
of any given year, I give in to the street level
divide of this fishing village world. On one side

of Lord Avenue two island black men rake and adjust
a Sunday morning beautiful flower bed. On the other side

• • •

three white men and three white women brake and adjust
their handlebar grips on bicycles, preparing to ride
wide into the *High Tide Guide* of St. Simon's. They

know Mullet Bay is on the way to vacation heaven.

At St. Simon's United Methodist Church there's
a statement, "Visitors Expected," and a question,

"Are you from Alaska?" No, I go unannounced

deeper into the lowcountry smell of Sunday morning
black island coffee. Look at me

walking now and talking to the air beneath the horizon
of Spanish moss–draped oak trees. The people here say

some of the trees look actually back at you. The people here
call it the Spirit-of-looking-back-trees. Sunday
morning on Lord knows what avenue now. How religious

can I get without calling myself to preach the gospel
according to John. My wife and daughter

in our rented room still, I imagine, asleep in dreams
of Sunday morning sunshine yellow and me reading
this sea island village like Sunday morning news. Maybe

I'll take a photograph and make myself out to be
Kodak Harrison looking

for the right angle to capture the composition
of Mrs. Abbott sitting quietly on her Sunday morning porch

dressed quite church like. She's colored native brown
in a coloring people island book. She was born here

. . .

when the coloring people owned every dirt road
in the village. "The whole island used to be colored

except," she tells me, "but now . . ." And she needs
to say no more

about Hazel's Café still standing since she was a child
dancing around a soul food table. At seventy years old
she fondly remembers playing

"Simon Says," in dirt-road front yards before
the legendary white horse came running down the beach
thundering up clouds that became hotel after hotel after
hotel. This was before, she remembers, roads became streets,

before "Points of Interest" and "Things to Do" were highlighted
in the *High Tide Guide*. Before it was necessary

to place a street sign on Lord Avenue, the people
knew

the color of Sunday morning sacred brown crayon. She,
Mrs. Abbott, wears a hat to service today. I tip mine
and walk in the direction of a dead end sign to see
if it really ends.

Knoxville, Tennessee

I always like summer
best
you can eat fresh corn
from daddy's garden
and okra
and greens
and cabbage
and lots of
barbecue
and buttermilk
and homemade ice-cream
at the church picnic
and listen to
gospel music
outside
at the church
homecoming
and go to the mountains with
your grandmother
and go barefooted
and be warm
all the time
not only when you go to bed
and sleep

Between Angels & Monsters

Short & baldheaded,
He paced the line of black boys
Flexing their muscles
& pointed to the ones he wanted.
Caged lions & tigers
Stared out of a lush
Green, eyes pulsing
Like lights from a distant city.

When he pointed to me,
I stepped closer to the elephants.
They moved like they had a history of work,
& knew where to place their feet
To not cave-in platforms
Loaded with stakes & tarp
Heavy as Hannibal's rafts
Tailgating on a river.

Soon we were hammering down steel pegs
& tying-off ropes, as they nudged pylons
Into place. A new world
Swelled under the big top.
Outside, a woman in stars-&-stripes bikini
Beckoned us. Near the aluminum trailers
A hundred colors heated the day
As women & men moved through doors,

. . .

A flash of bodies in bold windows.
A girl plucked a Spanish guitar
In the doorway of a tent
Where an armless man showed us
How he poured coffee & smoked
Chesterfields with his toes;
She placed a brush between his teeth
& he began painting a rose inside a bottle.

The baldheaded man was waving.
He gave each of us a free ticket
& a red T-shirt that said
The World's Greatest Circus.
We could hear the animal trainer's
Whip crack & bite into Saturday.
The smell of popcorn & chili dogs
Covered the scent of dung & dust.

A bouquet of flowers burst from a clown's trumpet.
We stood like obsidian panthers
In a corner of the white world.
It was as if our eyes had met
As she stepped off the highwire;
Her right foot hooked through a silver hoop—
Hanging like a limp flag
Over the invisible empire.

SONIA SANCHEZ

On Passing thru Morgantown

i saw you
vincent van
gogh perched
on those pennsylvania
cornfields communing
amid secret black
bird societies. yes.
i'm sure that was
you exploding your
fantastic delirium
while in the
distance
red Indian
hills beckoned.

Song of the South

What sense is it that this South has moved me?
All here is lovesweat and magnolia,
the way folks stare, then force their eyes to flee
the things my face may summon. How other

folks feel akin to this dark countenance,
unlike anything they've seen. How your hair,
if left to its own ways, will go from silk
back to cotton. How your bitter eyes dare

to remind me of why the blues tastes
bloody, why the sun always comes back home.
Down here, even in your arms, I am the face
dreamed of by a mother killing her own,

this land's buried desire, love's gold-eyed fear,
near answer to Uncle Remus' prayers.

————

This South has a way of spinning new scenes
of my familiar: I see your sunned face
in all things, wind through the silk-cotton tree,
I chant feathers on your neck. Funny the way

. . .

your full lips, bearing a briar patch of grief,
have become my sanctuary, and iambs
my shelter in these sonnets, so genteel,
no form is more Southern. Let's wade through white

fields for aloe and hold cool slivers to our
wounds letting juice drip bruise-purple as love.
Let's praise God below (for they are underground),
in a Song with no words but for low voices gone.

Let's go back, singing the South, descending green,
then red, then green again, the sun into the sea.

Our Natures Rise

hard core nights are so
erotic, a whiff of the
breeze is narcotic

Home (Running Man)

Miss Look:
Are you there?
Are you real?
Am I dreaming?
Is it really your voice?
Is it only the breeze?

You can walk from one end
To the other of my town
In a few heartbeats.

I guess it isn't even fair
To call it that.
It's Old Nancock, Virginia
On the Chesapeake,

Four or five buildings
Holding together
A dirt road.

Here are some things
The white folks
Let us keep:

A post office.
A general store.
A church.
A cemetery.

. . .

At night the old slaves
Dust themselves off
And rise from their graves

To catch a peek
Of the world
They never had.

They drift back
To the old shacks
We left standing,

Or to that place
In the swamp
Where their good luck
Turned hard.

From a speeding car
I'm sure it don't look
Like much:

Saw grass.
Seaweed.
Crickets.
Gull shit.
Everything you see
Says *keep going.*

There have always been
A few things
White folks
Won't bother with.

• • •

They drive by
And think of
Short ends
Of sticks.

To this day

You can still find
Chains
In the shacks.
It is a game we play
With our ghosts:

Their wrists
Are our wrists,
Our wrists
Are theirs,

And what's become
Of the key?

AL YOUNG

Landscape Mode

Overlooking the Cumberland River,
Clarksville, Tennessee,
early November 1996

In ancient Chinese paintings we see more sky than
earth, so when clouds hurry by in silver-gray
inkbursts of rolling readiness right along the river,

ripe with rain, rushing the road of time along,
pushing back light, belittling the black and white clarity
of Hollywood in its prime, the eye climbs down to greet

with shining gusto trees along the shore. Opryland
beyond the frame, the blue horizon hidden in a sea
of possibilities. And beyond this there's jazz: Jimmy Giuffre's

"Train on the River," stretched out strong like a pet cat
and that's that. But not quite. The poem paints
poorly what sketchers and colorists do best, The rest

should come out empty, allowing you to fill in your own
basic emptiness, your openness, your self-portrait
forged and catalogued; on quiet exhibit, on temporary loan.

Descended from clouds immensely more ancient than China,
you never quit becoming the background, the field in a sky
whose subtle earthiness sails over our heads altogether.

True Autumn

I return to the dead-end
street where I grew up, at the edge of
the county, at the foot of lavish
green hills, with dogwood- and magnolia-
plotted medians, where once a year,
my mother places a five-gallon bucket
of chitlins straight from the deepfreeze
next to the stove's warmth to thaw.
The long chain, slime-gray,
lovingly scrubbed clean of grit.
My mother says it's not true autumn
without eating them, as vital as blood-
rich colored oak leaves. As a kid
I loved the slurp of entrails
slicking my throat, but I never forgot
my white neighborhood friends' tables
set with bowls of lobster bisque
and baguette slices. Contained. Not all
food-juice mixing on the plate.
Over dinner my mother talked stories
of her father stringing hogs
for November slaughter as segue
to discussing black family mobility,
and my father drew imaginary lines
from stomach to mouth, a knife gutting
the hog body. How quickly matter
comes apart, as with words,
how to convey suburban two-acre lot,
where my family feasts on saucy delicacies
while trading superstitions about haints

and spirits and, in the next breath,
discussing protons penetrating solids.
How I used to crave no barrier
between me and other families. I'd pass
through brick and into beige safety—
no jellied pig's feet, no hot combs
smarting the ear, no smell
of oozing chitlins when it's near winter
and too cold to throw open windows
as we did. Each time the house filled
with their sweet stench, I'd cover my nose,
my mother always scolding,
"Some people never eat like this."

Driving South

We must have seen a hundred towns
with statues honoring the Confederate dead,
and at a telling distance,
the old slave block;
regional metaphors strong enough
to seduce my brother's Instamatic.

somewhere in South Carolina,
father drove the Dodge at a speed
slower than poured molasses,
and implored him to shoot General Lee.

TRUTH THOMAS

I Love It When You Call Me Big Country

4 Asha & Affrilachia

I'm on my way down home
wondering what draws me back

almost cicadalike, from cocoa Santa land
to Lynchaniggah City.

Hills scraped by dynamite fingers
watch the road, lifting me to Mammoth—

twelve miles from the K-Mart in Glasgow
a million miles from black hair care products.

Then, flipping digits, I hear it.
On 99.1 FM, Sentimental Sunday

Johnny walks the line, Loretta answers
daughter of coal mine.

Dolly says she'll always love me and
both Whitney and I understand.

Blue grass got in my locks
before Biggie did.

THE TWENTY-FIRST-CENTURY SOUTHERN RIFF AND SHOUT

Modern Lullabies for Planet Octavia

Ectopia

A stout bomb wrapped with a bow. With wear, you tear. It's true you sour
or rust. Some of us were sure you're in a rut. We bore your somber rub and
storm. You were true, but you rust. On our tour out, we tore, we two. You
were to trust in us, and we in you. Terribly, you tear. You tear us. You tell us
you're true. Are you sure? Most of you bow to the mob. Strut with worms,
strew your woe. So stow your tears, tout your worst. Be a brute, if you must.
You tear us most terribly. To the tomb, we rue our rust and rot. You tear. You
wear us out. You try your best, but we're bust. You tear out of us. We tear from
stem to stem. You trouble, you butter me most. You tear, but you tell us, trust
us to suture you.

Graphs: Photos from a Traveler

1
freesia
buds burst
freedom's flower
knotted, knitted
present past
tense torn
flesh flayed
browned back:
fat, thick

2
scents: burned maple
syrup, apple-smoked fat
back; sudden smell
trips, road slants
into histories'
pages frayed

3
hoary traveler's
camera shutters
open history,
keloidal territory,
tall tarred tales
swell, swelter

. . .

4
a swollen black
plum ripens
sour on the tree
burst flesh pulp
and circumstance:
klan ceremony

5
flesh festers
feathers: remnants
of chickened wing
plucked, fried
for picnicking
while *pickaninnies* fry

6
treed by coon dogs hunting
in an inglorious spot
america: proverbial chicken
couldn't cross
the road to freedom:
why? couldn't fly

7
from fated middle
passage: pustuled bark,
boats, scavenging
sharks, sea black
valley of dry sulphurous
bones: blacks caught in a crack

. . .

8
scour these sour snaps
shoots this flowering
this groove print
this last licorice lash
left this southern script
this hatred's hieroglyphs

9
this knot not a freedom
story this slavery post-
narrative: written on
the author, herself, no
edible fruit tree: bleeding
chokecherry, carcass, carrion

10
negative: *"nightmare begins"*
can't find what you can't see

11
no dream variations here
scanned visions of nightmare:
black as tarred skin, blinding
as bone-white feathers

CHERENE SHERRARD

Residual

after Kara Walker

Between our skins,
ink and paste, how
to loose the deep desires:
first finger the terrain of scars,
then prick the tempest of
my longing (the whip)
your need to wield it.

I Have Walked a Long Time

i have walked a long time
much longer than death that splinters
wid her innuendos.
my life, ah my alien life,
is like an echo of nostalgia
bringen blue screens to bury clouds
rinsen wite stones stretched among the sea.

> *you, man, will you remember me when i die?*
> *will you stare and stain my death and say*
> *i saw her dancen among swallows*
> *far from the world's obscenities?*
> *you, man, will you remember and cry?*

. . .

and i have not loved.
always
while the body prowls
the soul catalogues each step;
while the unconscious unbridles feasts
the flesh knots toward the shore.
ah, i have not loved
wid legs stretched like stalks against sheets
wid stomachs drainen the piracy of oceans
wid mouths discarden the gelatin
to shake the sharp self.
i have walked by memory of others
between the blood night
and twilights
i have lived in tunnels
and fed the bloodless fish;
between the yellow rain
and ash,
i have heard the rattle
of my seed,
so time, like some pearl necklace embracen
a superior whore, converges
and the swift spider binds my breast.

you, man, will you remember me when i die?
will you stare and stain my death and say
i saw her applauden suns
far from the grandiose audience?
you, man, will you remember and cry?

saturday & a glimpse of sunday

1
day breaks
spilling a mass of yellow
across the sky

yawning
ginger wonders
if the goddesses will make omelets

2
on the way to the trash can
a banana
stricken with melanoma
asks me to peel her skin back
insisting her fruit is not yet bruised

an hour later
a small bread loaf
collapses in mourning

3
up to our necks in bath water
sweetened with peppermint
ginger sings me
"ne me quitte pas"
causing the wall tiles
to break away one by one
revealing a young nina simone
serenading the eiffel tower

. . .

4
driving to the flea market
with a trunk full of homemade jewelry
t-shirts & sugar scrubs
we spot death crossing the highway
carrying two winged children

5
at a booth adjacent to us
an elderly chinese man selling pecan rolls
yawns without covering his mouth
& out comes cigar smoke
in the shape of a dragon

6
night falls
breaking both legs
& a collarbone

somewhere in the distance
wolves cry for help

later
while ginger sleeps
demons fall
through the bags beneath my eyes
slide down my cheeks
land on my pillow
& act out a rape scene

7
day breaks
as if someone stuck a pin in it

outside our window
cars run over their reflections

Haiku 142005

Petals hide from heat
A shy southern clitoris
Afraid beyond thighs.

community day

1

the sun laid on top of us
coating our bodies in her heavy breath
that condensed.
balling up into angry droplets
that stood and refused to become rivulets.
i heard some folks mumble
we was too black to be out
here in this bare-ass sun
gettin' blacker by the minute.
some folks hair was sweatin' back.
a few warnings were passed around
about niggas and how they get to fightin'
when they get too hot.

2

bourgeois niggas like us
can't sit through black talent shows
cause soon as little maleasha
sings the third version of
greatest love of all
we start rolling our eyes
placing bets on how many times
martin luther the king
gets mentioned
and when that young, young girl comes out
dressed as that old, old slave
to recite *mother to son* . . .

. . .

meanwhile
in boca raton
there are beach houses
that look like sugar candy;
pastel, delicious.
so clean.
the maid is named lupe;
there is a helipad,
and the señor? he brings in dopa
for diñero.

3
in a place where they cut down all the trees
and name the streets after them
i once heard a lady with a french last name
complain that all the other women
in her neighborhood
had no imagination.
she had to go way out of
town to find wallpaper
they couldn't copy.
and let's not even talk about
how many blazers showed up
in driveways
after she bought hers!

. . .

4
here her little self is pitiful
black and small
smaller than our hate
much less impressive than
our wounds that the sun
and complacency have baked
until they are hard
all the way through
her desperate chin straining at some impossible angle
her plea: "i am somebody!"

5
outside they are protesting.
right outside of the whitey convention.
their multitude of sons are broadcast on tv
the edges of their mouths froth—
they are rabid for revolution.
they are so tired of me and grandmama
having to be black and poor.
they are tired of our shows
and our liquor stores with accompanying churches
our negro poems.
they are sick of the hot, hot sun and how it presses us.
they plead with their daddies
"bump up our inheritance
so we can help them."

Afronauts

for Adam Banks

Night's nightmarish record-vinyl darkness,
        wild stylus outrageous and rooted in reflector.
A pillbox of plantations, even bigger cotton,
        and wades of shock
folk like us wave off. Unsleeved plastic,
        both flat black sides,
        a single and a signal

double conscious as stereo,
        Afro-modernity's unfinished and triangular,
soul-auction-troped ear—less land than less,
        the not-yet-black Black Atlantic's
crisscrossed under dynamic traffic.
        Phat black smiles, phat black similes,
        and phat black miles.

Any number of syncretic speakers spanking
        and spankers speaking
—unchartable *r*hythm*r*hythm*r*hythm
        going round the needle's sharklike patience.
The universe, a panasonic dance floor,
        plaid-about stars. Well what,
        if not memory, is orbit?

. . .

Section Eights, double-platinum ones,
      black minds already know,
all economically all diasporically looped.
      Shoes, unlike the sun, always OFF.
Pelvic dress and walk,
      the sweetest badass bounce.
      Ohh! Space memory

of running for one's life
      overboard into race.

We Real Crunk

after Gwendolyn Brooks

We real crunk. We
Buy junk. We

Walk slow. Wear
Pants low. We

Sling rocks. Run
From cops. We

Get laid. Die
From AIDS.

JARVIS Q. DeBERRY

Diovan HCT 160MG

A nurse once said to me, "Baby, you nervous?"
I shook my head back and said, "No."
She again pumped up the sphygmomanometer.
"How old are you, baby?" "Twenty-two."

High blood pressure is so James Evans.
The want ads with eviction on his mind.
It's corner store pig's feet, ears, maw, and souse.
It's Morton's raining down on the poor.

It's dialysis centers that look like prisons,
Big Daddy's stroke. Then his silence.
It's "Bless this food for the nourishment of our bodies."
It's expecting a whole lot of God.

It's the stubborn niggerness I cannot tame.
Not even with a fancy degree.
Not with marathons, salads, and meatless diets.
Not even with bootstrap conviction.

Three the Hard Way

after *Their Eyes Were Watching God*

Grandma didn't want me
to hoe from can't see
in the morning till can't see
at night. It wasn't Logan

Killicks she wanted me to marry.
It was protection. It was sixty acres
of cotton and sweat. It was
walking into the house and waiting

for love to begin. Noticing poems
didn't grow in his mouth, his fingers
sobering up in my long
black hair just two months

after our tongues came
closer than words. It was his
long flat head, fat back.
I was a mystery. I wanted

to want him. I don't want him
to do all de wantin'. Didn't want him
to tell me to chop wood. Shoot,
the earth drinks urine and perfume

•   •   •

just the same. So I cut his coffee,
fried the hoecake, glazed the sow-
belly. I ain't gonna ache. I ain't
gonna wait. Gone.

2

Sittin' on the porch blooming Eatonville. Sunlight
sneaking through the slats, taking
a breather after traveling for a spell. Citified
Georgia Joe gone. I sent my feelings
to the funeral. Some think

I'm the reason. Questionizin' him.
But I had an inside and an outside,
and I knew how to hang them
in different closets. Seal Brown
Joe, Eatonville mayor. Mouth
so big the Mississippi shivered
when he spoke—we lived in Florida:
You ain't got no more business
wid uh plow than a hog
has got wid uh holiday. I couldn't be

around the gum grease, had to rub
tongues with the high muckety mucks,
sit with my wrists and hands
folded while he shoved rules
down my throat. Wouldn't let me

get in the conversations
on the porch; wouldn't let me
roll in the laughter; would breathe
for me if he could get his
air in my nose. Portly

· · ·

when I met him and now fat
slid across his ribs. But he was
insulting me: *You getting old
as Methuselah, rump hanging to your knees.*
My calves were fat with answers

I had kept to myself. I peeled back
my tongue: *Joe, you pull
down your britches, and the wind
covers its eyes.* The men's laughter
made his ankles explode. He

pointed that stogie, that fat finger
of spinach, lifted his left hand so high
the sky flinched: *Ah see one
thing and understand ten.*

*You see ten and understand
one.* There was silence,
the quiet of knives. I yanked that do-
rag off my head—Joe's hand-
cuff—let my hair tickle
my hips on the way home. Joe moved
downstairs. Love left the bedroom, sat
in the parlor, made small talk
with the customers. The Mississippi
didn't get the jitters no more.

3
I am coffee. I am cream. Mrs. Turner says
I'm a featured woman, ain't got no liver
lips and flat nose. But I'm in love

with the coo in midnight. Teacake
I'm afraid of misunderstanding
more than death, waking up in a bed

· · ·

wet with conversations and sex.
My fingernails, my breasts, the ball
of my foot is one slow love

song only you know how to sing.
You learned me ecstasy. You
learned me jealousy. Love

so good it throbbed when I seen muscle
-butt Nunkie out in the cotton
trying to grab that giggle

between your legs. Trying to
snatch my laughter. I bought it,
paid for it, spread the wings

between my legs for it. Lake
Okeechobee's bosom spilling out
her bra, muddy jugs big enough to feed

a small country. Damn dog sharpened
its teeth on a hurricane. Teacake

pulled out his knife, killed it,
but not before that mutt bit
the swagger in his cheekbone.

4
How do you aim a gun
at love? Is it as simple
as fishing and checkers. Half
gods sip wine and buttercups. Real

. . .

Gods drink blood. Teacake, I see you
kissing that pillow. *How come
you can't sleep with me,
woman?* His tongue

flopping like a nervous sock, him reaching
for a piece of the river, choking
on a cup of water that's soft
and wrong. *I need a quart of coon*

dick. I'd whisper in the moon's
ear if it would save you, Teacake.
*What you want in that bedroom?
Come back here!* That pistol

under the pillow. A six-shooter
with five hungry chambers,
we only gonna eat one meal
this evening. Fear and hope. Click.

Hope and fear. Click.
How do I aim a gun
at love? *Teacake there is a tiger
struttin' 'cross your eyelashes.* I whipped

up the Winchester, winced, and shot.
He poured his body, that lanky
love song, into my lap. Why I had to put
a bullet in the music, Sugar? Lord,

if you'll let me, I'm gonna
unbutton the house,
let Tea's last breath crawl

• • •

out the window. Bootyny! Sop-de-Bottom!
Coodemay! Stew Beef! SSSh. This sadness
is animal, killing me through Teacake.
NNNNNNNNNo? You loved me
in blue. I couldn't wear it right
now. I looked down. Mrs. Turner
would say I was staring
at the dark. But no, my eyes,

my eyes were watching God.

Lawn Jockey

Recently, I've been having trouble distinguishing
human beings from lawn ornaments.
— Wayne Koestenbaum

This instance is one of those instances when
a joke goes over well with the audience,
with most of the audience.
Perhaps you cannot tell,
because of the decibels of pale laughter,
that I am in the room.

Not being able to distinguish humans
from lawn ornaments is the kind of mistake
on which our nation is founded—
not in theory, but in practice—the kind of
humorous ineptitude that the Führer might
have shared with comrades over beer.

If I were to put on my riding pants and boots,
stand outside your apartment building (no
doubt luxurious by a poor man's judgment)
with a lantern and a big grin awaiting your
return, would that help?
Or would that complicate the problem?

LYRAE VAN CLIEF-STEFANON

Poem for Amadou Diallo

> *history*
> *has taught us much about fame and its*
> *inevitable tomorrow.*
> — *Lucille Clifton*

This is your fifteen minutes
of fame. So violently sudden, it caught you
peering at the contents of your life
from outside your Bronx apartment window.
How quickly the vestibule reflects
fame's pop and flare and flash;
echoes with its din—the rapid-fire clap
unexpected as applause.

Your body can't help its poses as four nightriders fire like paparazzi,
twisting you with each shot. You are almost dancing—
reaching for what you don't know about America and identity—
your spine shifted, slips. How swiftly you fall. It is impossible to stand.

Your own blood fills your chest until you are nothing
but poems and petals left on Wheeler Street
and your mother's courtroom silence
as she learns to hold her heart.

Big Thicket: Pastoral

Jasper, Texas

to Big Thicket
a KRAK! is a buck
shot   to Big
Thicket KRAK!
is a stick broke
KRAK! headlights
staggering home
the road kills   buck KRAK!
to Big Thicket we go
we go to sticks
to stick bucks
hot   drink drink
heads light   stagger
ing the road
long the trees   long
the creek KRAK!
stick broke   light
kills   we go we go
to Big Thicket
to home on a kill
buckshot KRAK! stag
gered by the white
tits   head light
to Big Thicket
buck on each
pickup   staggering
what you looking at
the white tits   stick

346

broke KRAK! buck
broke KRAK! the white
stick Big Thick
et long the trees
long the creek
drink staggered
broke white kill
the buck staggering
home KRAK!
the trees pick up   we
go we go
gone   to Big Thicket
what you doing here buck
stick to home
KRAK! stick broke
huffhuffgogo white light
break the trees   break
for home   long the road
home   whites homing on
we   huffhuffgogo
buckshot KRAK! KRAK!
KRAK! KRAK! we go we
go gone   to Big Thicket
long the Huff Creek
the rushes in the drink
hothead whites
what you think
you are   buck
huff KRAK! huff KRAK!
is fists boots bone KRAK! a
stick broke   buck stick
in the rushes   buck back
in the rushes   put them
back on   put them back
on   buck
head in the rushes
what you think

347

in the rushes   put them
back on   put them back
on   to Big Thicket we go
to Huff Creek-head
hot   we go to head
staggering long the trees
the staggered creek-head
the rushes KRAK! a
stick broke   the creek breaks
the hot light   to Big Thicket
we go we go gone
to white huff to bucks shot
to long road home we go we
go we gone to Big Thicket
to Huff Creek Road   of drunk
pick-ups   road kill stag
gering bucks
hot   drunk   head
light rushes Huff
Creek Road   pickup
rushes drunk and screech
ing brakes   Huff Creek
rode by drunk
and screeching whites
what you what
you what you to Big Thicket
we go we go gone
KRAK! is a buck
shot KRAK! is fists boots
bone KRAK! the road kills KRAK!
a broke stick long the
staggered creek it go it go
on

Dressing Down

to "Shirley Q. Liquor" aka Chuck Knipp

After the drag show,
Afro wig tossed on the pale dummy's head,
you scour the tar moon mask,
revealing pink putty underneath.
It's still you—Miss Thang—
no matter what you apply or conceal.

Clown of a desperate circus,
you traded glamour for nasty tricks,
dethroning your mammy for dollars
that will never cover so much debt,
unraveling years she lost
loving you for a living.

When you're gay in Dixie,
sometimes the only way to be like daddy
is to hate like him—
wrap a Confederate skirt around your waist
in twisted tribute,
offer a neck other than your own

and hope your brothers laugh instead of shoot.

Elegy for the Mad Brother @ Borders

(and Barnes, Books-A-Million, Waldenbooks, B. Dalton, so on and so forth)

They let that white kid stick Juicy Fruit
in the African / American (colored section) books.
Smiled as his dad charged
not one but four Yanni CDs,
Windows® For Dummies,
and a double row of chocolates.

The brunette
who unleashed her
Chihuahua, they let
her in,
watched as she
lugged a pancake stack of books
into a dim corner. The dog even fetched one,
its small sharp teeth
sinking in hardback
as if through grapefruit skin.
She just rolled out her laptop.
How gushy they all were
to oblige, to perform title searches,
to give her a phone cord
so she could jack on to the Net.
Even brought her an espresso
on the house.

. . .

But you? Yo,
they did a double-take
when the poetry
hit the counter. Jayne. Emily.
Ntozake. Sylvia. Asked to see
your license when you presented
your MasterCard. Like, yeah,
the bookstore
is the first place you'd go,
not to Circuit City
for the new computer
no one would believe you could afford.
And not to Expedia (dot com)
for a one-way to Fiji.
With the price of oil,
why not a gas station?
And when you stayed quiet,
politely refused to prove yourself
and walked away,
they made an obnoxious comment
about you and Dickinson.

REGINALD FLOOD

Poem for June Jordan

It was only after stone-cold dead Eula Love
could we hear the word, understand the way
you stole back flesh to mesh rage and beauty
into ritual and rhyme that righteously defrays
any doubt that what happens on this white page
can carve out hard songs of hope and freedom
like a poem about an old black woman
with a knife being ushered into the kingdom
by sixteen bullets from two of LAPD's finest
responding to a disturbance call from Metro,
two men, six feet plus, fearing for their lives—this woman,
five-six, flowered robe, matching house slippers, that never let go
(they claimed) of that kitchen knife, so they reloaded
to fire again and again while she lay there prone
on her front yard, eyes closing on a city that would soon
soon explode into another third-world war zone.

Eula was somebody's daughter, cousin, friend, lover.
She had those sweet nights when it was *amaze me baby*
with a man or woman who for that one moment
could see only her, nothing more than her in all that crazy
delicious sweaty confusion that stops the damn world,
halts it—till you catch your breath and try to bridle desire
hands, fingers, tongue: all the limbs still trembling,
certain now that any fool denying love exists is a liar.

•   •   •

Like lots of folks in South Central, Eula probably belonged
to a Mississippi or Georgia club, rubbing the scars of that lash
each summer taking the bus back to where it's hello honey
how you doing Miss Love, linking sharecropper's past
to the surrender celebrated in another black folks' garden
collards, bush beans, sweet potatoes and melons,
neat rows sprouting in her Compton backyard, dragging
one of the few things from the South worth stealing.
Busload of old folks that risked everything to leave
cruising back in air-conditioned comfort
four decades later with grand babies to the home place,
knowing that this time they are wanted
for more than just their backs for a season,
twelve to fourteen a day, minus seed, food, and rent,
leaving barely a living until the planting begins again,
hungry all the time—thinking damn: this is what freedom meant?

There were only broken bricks, busted glass, and jagged concrete,
small mountains of anger without bones until you, June Jordan,
made fire songs by putting flesh on all the lies and deceit
so that we could see Watts, Soweto, Harlem, and Stone Mountain
in the bullet holes and body of that old black lady
passing to the other side in a housecoat, bleeding out on her front lawn,
only slippers and dignity on: the cops calling her stone crazy
but the real madness: a dried-out garden and one more sister gone.

The phrase "amaze me baby" is taken from June Jordan's "A Poem about
Police Violence."

apathy no more

/written the day it rained in post–new york/

red, white, and blue banners
bruise brown brothas wit their backlash;
see them streetwalking in the garb of a war
western apathy has too long ignored;
see them bleeding the sweat of accusation
as prejudice points its fanatical finger
in the name of fathers of undermined freedom

amid media descriptions of what war looks like
is what war smells like,
is the stench of what war costs
and what war gains;
when brown skin adopts a civilized home,
even mother liberty mocks and blames
as she nurses palestinian oppression
and cradles diallo deadened by swat teams

it aint easy bein anti-imperialist
when christian militants celebrate reaction
because there is nothing to replace the fallen
and angry fists cannot hold this burning hate
that organizes itself in a puddle of warped patriotism

. . .

it rained in new york today;
water seeped beneath the soot
of injured infrastructures and broken homes
to wet the throats of the screaming dead,
to quench the thirsts of questioning children;
and if there is a God,
the blood will wash wall street clean of these days
that could not happen in this self-sacred place
where phallic pride and a rotting apple
are reasons to rally in this season to cry

it is raining
as the media seduces us
with whispers of
go get the brown

Gentleman

        And he says to me, you're such a nice guy,
Meaning to say I'm too nice sometimes
For my own good, too nice sometimes to be real and
Spontaneous. I'm a Southerner, I remind him.
I grew up in a church family. I grew up black and a male.
I grew up hiding I was "funny."

I say, in an episode of *The Simpsons*, the family finds itself
In Africa at the top of a long waterfall.
Down below lie two paths, a lush, calm, and sunny one
To the right, and a turbulent, bleak one to the left,
And the scene goes back and forth
Between these possibilities twice to heighten the humor.
Homer chooses the right one, of course,
But just before they reach the fork, a wind comes along
And steers them the other way.

I say, Being nice is serious business—
Someone is forever poised at a precipice
That is ugly and threatens to take us off course,
And the only rescue from the graceless drop
Is the chance to decide what happens next.

Eartha Takes the Old Woman Shopping for Red Shoes

because neighbors
don't speak
and never stay put

because the weather
dies slowly in scenic
skies   because

for once the heat
stays longer than geese
because you let too many

moons change
your mind
and buying

red shoes means
exceptional days
when clocks

run uphill and back
to better days
when red

oh bloody youth
all fire and brass
when red

. . .

lasted whole nights
after you've seen
too many sunsets

where laughter spools
into primary colors
days all smudge-proof

full of crisp
seasons and moons
waxing full

and Eartha whispers
over your shoulder
if somebody asks

just take them
back to '53
or '68 if pushed

when rock and roll
was the real thing
and we were slick

as kittens and purred
long black legs ending
in patent red shoes

One for Strom

Strum the banjo.
Strom is dead.
   Tickertape, tickertape,
   Soul parade.
     Grits-cooking woman
    Lower your head.
       Strom is dead, y'all.
       Strom is dead.
         Bible school dropout,
        Scripture's been read.
           Bull Connor's waiting.
          (No more hoses)
          The fire instead.

Now

I park the car because I'm happy,
because if everyone parked we'd have a street party,
because the moon is full—
it's orange, the sky is closer
and it would be wrong to drive into it.
This is summer's first day—
everyone is hanging out,
women walk by in their bodies so mellow
I feel I'm near a friend's house.

The small white flakes of the headlights
sweat for a second on the storefronts.
In the windows, darkened afterhours,
A reflection stares back
looking more like me than me.
I reach to touch
and the reflection touches me.
Everything is perfect—
even my skin fits.

. . .

Hanging out,
the taillights of the turning cars
are fires, going out—
are the spaces of roses flowered
deeper in themselves. I close my eyes
and am flowered deeper in myself.
Further up the street a walking figure
I can't make out, a face
behind a bag of groceries, free arm swinging
in the air the wave of a deep red
fluid shifting to and fro.

At the vegetarian restaurant
I see it's Michael the Conga Drummer—
been looking for him 2 months.
He asks me, "What's happening."
I love his fingers.
When we shake hands I mix his grip
with the curve of my father's
toting cantaloupe in the house from the market.
We are two griots at an intersection.
I answer him in parable:
The orange that I've been carrying
is some luminous memory, bursting,
bigger than my hand can hold,
so I hand him half.

NIKKY FINNEY INTERVIEWS LUCILLE CLIFTON

Columbia, Maryland
January 13, 2006

NF: There is an old saying: A daughter comes from her mother, but through her grandmothers. Do you think that's true?

LC: The saying in our family was always that we were a family of strong women and weak men. I find that may well be true, even though I wouldn't want my grandsons to know this. I think I am a product of both. My maternal grandmother was a complete nut but she was still strong. My mother—who is the angel in my life—was very much in her way a strong woman. She might have seemed not so but she was. People mistake gentleness for weakness and that is a mistake. I think I am also a product of the stories I know. I don't know a lot about my mother's family other than that grandmother. My father's grandmother and mother were the women I knew more about. But perhaps that old saying is true. They are indeed the women I identified with.

NF: I've been thinking a lot about the journey of your mother, Thelma Sayles. A poet in her own right, yes?

LC: Yes. Oh yes.

NF: It is my understanding that she wrote and read to you preciously and often.

LC: Yes, she recited poems to me. I've recited my mother's poems that she recited often to me. "Abu Ben Adam," "The House by the Side of the Road," Paul Laurence Dunbar, whom she loved. Paul Laurence Dunbar's and my birthday are the same date. Different years, of course. [*laughs*]. I would sit on my mother's lap until she died. I was twenty-one when she died. I never thought that was odd. Here is this big pregnant—I was huge with my first child—and she would rock me and recite Paul Laurence Dunbar and other poems.

NF: I don't know another Black woman poet who had a working poet for a mother. It sounds as though your mother's personal affection for language and for poetry prepared your ears for being a poet in this world. I see what she gave you as almost a second birth.

LC: Oh my. Oh, yes indeed. I hadn't thought about that. Yes, yes indeed. Absolutely. It was! It was. You know what is interesting too? My mother was a great numbers player, as were the other women in the neighborhood, and oddly enough when I was a kid in elementary school, at lunch I would go home and go across the street to the number runner's house and take calls on his phone for him. I bet there are a lot of women poets who went to college but never had this experience [*laughs*]. Her number was 254 and that was our address at one point. Well, when I went in for my kidney transplant, I knew I would be OK for two reasons: one, because my hospital number was 425, and the other was because my mother couldn't finish writing her poems. I have a poem called "Fury" about my mother burning her poems. And I knew she would not allow me to not be able to finish. I really do believe she guides me on not allowing me to not do my work. She was amazing—I have a short story called "The Magic Mama"—a very short story. I think you're right. She did prepare me to hear the language, because to this day, I'm still a very aural person.

NF: Our anthology is entitled *The Ringing Ear*. The name is borrowed from Forrest Hamer's fine poem "Middle Ear." It's here in the ear for us as poets isn't it? Poetry is so intimately a sound-based art.

LC: I really think people forget about sound in poetry. When I was at Columbia [University], I taught a course on hearing poems. My mother's poems were very traditional, iambic pentameter verse. I remember I would be writing a poem and my mother would say, "Ah, baby, that ain't no poem! Let me show you how to write a poem." Then she would rhyme something. I do probably have a good ear for language and I do think poetry is listening and hearing based. "Lias, Lias, Bless de Lawd / Don't you know the day's abroad / If you don't get up, you scamp / Dey'll be trouble in this camp!" And the many things she would say. My father would recite the Bible. He knew the Bible very well, but my father couldn't write. Just hearing the language. I didn't purposely say, "I want to hear the tones!" Hearing and listening just became part of who I am.

NF: In the bones?

LC: Absolutely, in the bones.

NF: Our anthology is a collection of poetry with southern leanings and connections. You were raised in Depew, New York, but your family had deep southern roots, as did many Black people of that era. I think of songs from my girlhood, southern songs, games we played in the yard: "3-6-9 . . . the goose drank wine . . . the monkey chewed tobacco on the streetcar line." There was so much poetry laced inside those patty-cake yard girl games. Did "Miss Mary Mack" make the journey North into your girlhood?

LC: I did grow up in Depew, and I was five when we left, and in Depew the only other Black females, young ones, were my oldest sister, who was seven years older than I and who is dead now, and my youngest sister, who is only six months and two days younger than I. So I was a very solitary kind of kid. But I always loved music. I've always loved and not questioned my intuition about things. I do question my intellect a fair amount but not my intuition. Lane, my sister, we would play this thing called "Dumb School." And, yes, we would play "Miss Mary Mack, Mack, Mack, all dressed in black, black, black." People haven't really looked at games and such enough, I don't think. My mother was Sanctified. We were embarrassed about this. My father was Baptist, so I heard the preaching constantly. People ask me about my poetic background and I say, "Oh, well, it's Reverend Meriweather of course." Absolutely! The sound of *that*. I do think the ear is underrated. When people began to study poetry in schools—and I may be wrong because I do teach it myself—they stopped listening to poems and began seeing them as only matters of the eye. And of course it isn't just that, but when we start attaching only the eye we attach that to the intellect only.

NF: And detach . . .

LC: Yes, and detach from the world of sound. A poet's song and music. All of those things. The dangerous thing there though—and my students get mad at me—not really mad, but they think I am such a "terrible person"—because I don't think Smokey Robinson was a great poet. I'm sorry—"Smoke" will rhyme anything. There is a mistake made even in this relishing of sound because you can go too far in anything. White kids always ask about Bob Dylan. I think Stevie Wonder approaches poetry, *approaches*. I think Simon and Garfunkel *approach* poetry. Which doesn't mean I don't care about them as musicians. I do indeed. I love Stevie. But . . .

NF: Every rhyme does not a poem make . . .

LC: No indeed.

NF: Could we go back to the little girl for a minute? Could you use some of those concise, evocative, Lucille Clifton grown-woman-poet words to describe Lucille Sayles, the girl-poet at eight or nine? You mentioned her solitariness.

LC: I was very, very much that kind of solitary person. I have some poems I'm trying to write right now about Lucille. I'm trying to recapture the girl . . . you get to an age where you start thinking, "What ever happened to her?" I'm writing some things from the 1940s and early '50s trying to think about what I was like before this poetry thing—this public thing—descended, because by the time I was published, I was thirty-something years old and had six children.

NF: Yes, that's the little human being I'm wondering about, that little girl in your memoir, *Generations,* who remembers her father walking to Buffalo to buy a dining room suite when no Black people owned or bought such things in Buffalo, New York. You describe this so vividly in those pages, recalling your father paying that dollar fifty a week for fifty years and recalling the owner of the furniture shop, Sam Pitterman.

LC: Yes! Yes! Oh my! His name was Sam Pitterman and my father's name was Sam also. He and Daddy would sit on the porch and talk and talk. These were not people who would have met each other in the street.

NF: He called your father Sam or Samuel and . . .

LC: Yes, and Daddy had to call him Mr. Pitterman even though they had the same first name. I hated this so much. So much. My sister and I both hated it so much.

NF: But you saw this and it made an impression on you as a girl.

LC: Yes, that little girl watching this and other things go on and drawing conclusions and trying to figure out what it meant. Everywhere there are connections. Everything is connected. I sincerely believe that. I've always been a person who tried to figure out, How is this connected? How is this connected generally and then how is it connected to me? What is it that I should understand? What should I be aware of?

NF: I was reading some old interviews that you had given over the years and in one of them you recall the first time hearing and being called the word "nigger," and I'll never forget what your response to that was. It was such an important response.

LC: Yes, it taught me not to believe them. That word certainly had nothing to do with me. That was not who I was.

NF: After understanding this, you also went on to say something like, "Well, from now on I'm going to have to question everything they say."

LC: Yes, absolutely. After that I had to check all this out.

NF: And you've been doing that kind of "checking everything out" ever since.

LC: All my life. All—my—life. When they say *"this"* now, I know I better check it out, which is why I would have made such a good research person, really, because I will check it out. I will.

NF: It's such a blessing for a poet to have this, to have this deep curiosity about things in general and then to apply it specifically to the work in their life.

LC: Maybe so. One of those blessing-curses! I don't know. It's like—excuse me—but I sometimes go off in tangents because tangents are so wonderful—aren't they so wonderful?—but I got very interested in the Black Madonna, who in Europe in particular is a very revered person. So I started reading, and in one of the places I read that it was the smoke from the candles that were burned around the Madonna that turned her face black. That was one of the explanations. You see—so then my first thing was to ask, Well, OK, then what about her hands? See, you've got to check all these things out. So I have my own little belief system. It's called Lucille's Belief System. Just to check it out for myself. When people say *this* is because of *this*, I have to find it out for myself. I just have to.

NF: I think this can be applied in so many different ways to poetry and poetry writing. I tell my students so often that they stop too soon in their personal fretting-creation process. They see something that looks and sounds wonderful, a word or a sound, and they are so enthralled with it that they just end it there instead of stretching it out just a little farther, pushing through their own delight and wondering about it just a little bit more. They don't take it as far as it can go. They think the first tingle is the end, when it's only the beginning.

LC: One of the poems I'm writing now is a poem called "Aunt Jemima," and it's in the voice of a little section I'm going to call "Colored Women." It has not only African American icons and women, but Hebrew icons and women. You know my thing is . . . well, this is my life I'm talking about here. This is the kind of wide sweep I've had in my life. What I've done in my work all my life with different kinds of images and icons. In "Aunt Jemima" it begins: "White folks think I remind them of home," and then she talks about being in the kitchens and so forth. But she's homeless! Aunt Jemima was homeless. She says, "I have no home other than this shelf / and what I long for is my own house / my own nephews and nieces. My own home." Something like that. But just taking that thought, that icon, that image to the next step, just pushing it just a little bit more, gave me that other line of thought to travel.

NF: You were talking at Furious Flower II just casually in between the reading of the poems, and you said, "Oh, I have such a quirky mind." I thought, "That is the part to protect."

LC: That's kind of hard to talk about in a way. One of my great assets is that I'm not educated at all. Which does not mean that I don't know anything. You'd be making a great mistake if you thought I was stupid. I'm not stupid. I can be naive and dumb, but stupid? No. Just never having learned how you are supposed to be.

Writing poems is not something I was taught. I learned it. It just seemed natural. I saw my mother doing it, of course. It's just a way I approach things. It's a part of who I am.

I hesitate very much to say my life would be impoverished very much if I didn't write poetry. That's not the high point of my life. I have six children. I have grandchildren. And I'm looking around at all times. You never know. It certainly is a part of what makes me whoever I am.

NF: Maybe it's that private, quirky Lucille place, protected, that allows you to be in all those other places so well.

LC: Yes, maybe so. Maybe so.

NF: How you *think* about something is so important?

LC: And how you *feel* about something is so important.

NF: What is a sixteen-year-old Black girl from Depew, New York, thinking or feeling when she leaves home and enters Howard University, such a world away, and decides to not major in anything safe, Black and female and well-trodden, but instead chooses drama as her major?

LC: Oh, I loved the theater.

NF: Even before Howard?

LC: Oh yes. An English teacher in high school took me to see somebody's one-man show, and this someone did Charles Dickens. Oh, what was his name? Such a long time ago. And I just thought it was the most wonderful thing. Because as *me*, I was so shy and it was so difficult for me. But as Lady Whoever. . . . It was very cool. I loved—I don't want to say "pretending" because I don't pretend that well. But getting into someone else's possibilities, yes, I can do that. This also helps me in poems because I can do other people's characters. I can do dramatic monologue. I can feel into someone else how it must be for them. I don't know how I do this but I do it. I do it a lot. Someone said to me once that what I do is find "the myth in the human and the human in the myth." And so in my poetry I can speak in the voice of Mary because Mary was a woman.

I'm a great newspaper person because I'm nosey. We're nosey people in my family. One of the things that bothers me is everybody is trying to fix the events in the world, but it's the people that need help. Do something about the people. I think everybody has had a nervous breakdown. I really do.

NF: That takes me to my question about New Orleans. It is eight months after Katrina, the broken levees and the abandoned people on rooftops. I'm thinking of Ma' Carline, your grandmother, walking from New Orleans to Virginia in the 1840s. Any thoughts about New Orleans?

LC: I have a new poem about New Orleans. I don't know it [by heart] just yet. It's about this woman who has found a baby floating in the river during the worst of the moments there. She wants to announce to the people in New Orleans that the baby is found. And she never will forget the baby. Whose baby? She doesn't know. What baby? Not sure. What matters is only that *the baby* is found. What happened in New Orleans is no coincidence. It isn't so much that people are trying to mess up the lives of Black folk. It is their ignorance. People have lost the capacity to care for other people. People are so wrapped up in fixing events that they have forgotten about the people. Which president's wife was it that said, "Well, they didn't have much in the first place?" I mean, that's crazy talk. Our lives as Black people are quite isolated lives. Too often what we pay attention to is the look of a thing and not what's behind it.

NF: There are so many riveting lines in *Generations*. First, there is your grandmother in one chapter naming you "Genius." Then there is a line in another chapter where you were told, "Get away, get away! Leave this place for someplace better." Is there anyplace left to go where young Black people may take their genius so that it may properly bloom?

LC: Actually, no there isn't. Who was it—Eliot?—who talks about returning to where he was and knowing it for the first time? I think we must jolt ourselves out of our comfort zones, what we are used to. My hometown was Polish. My family was the Black family there. This was a group of very interesting people. This taught me early that family means everybody. I think it's important for us to see something else in our lives.

NF: And that must go hand in hand with your grandmother saying out loud as her friends left Virginia and moved to New York City, "Oh I just wanna see some things." I remember my own mother and grandmother saying some version of this often in their lives. This desire to have a full life was always present in the throats of Black women who raised me.

LC: Yes. Well, that's something felt a lot in life. When my children were all very young, my litany was, "These same-y days. These same-y days." Something in us knows that this ain't all. I don't know if men have that at all. It's so interesting because I've always wondered about people who always wanted to go and see Paris and Rome and they haven't seen Pasadena. You know? I wanted to see Memphis. I've read in every state including Alaska and Hawaii. I've read in Tel Aviv and Jerusalem. I have not been on the African continent. I feel that I will. Because I don't accept others' view of things. I do have to go and see for myself. I have always been this way.

NF: Were you setting out to be a poet?

LC: Never thought about it. It never occurred to me. Never thought about publishing. I just wrote poems. I loved Robert Hayden. He was so clear. He was so musical. I like the music of the American tongue.

NF: People call you a minimalist. Do you think that is true?

LC: No. I don't think about it. These labels and things are generally given after the fact when people are trying to figure out where to put you. I find myself put in a lot of different places. It seems I have lived several lives in several places. I use the language I use because I'm not appealing just to the intellect. What I'm trying to do is use language to its greatest possibility.

I read a bad review of my work about two weeks ago. My girls were saying, "Mom, stop, don't do it." It was from a long time ago. The reviewer said, "She's a wise person and all that, but she's no poet." I came home. I'm a Cancer, OK. I wept into my pillow. I wondered why had I thrown away my life. The conventions of poetry that people seem to always expect—well—I hope that I try to do poetry with all that I am and I hope that some of it somewhere reaches someone in all that they are. I write about what it means to be human. To me one of the great poets of all time is Stanley Kunitz. Stanley talks about what it means to be human in this place in this time. I once asked him, "What did I give up for this poetry thing? What did I give up for this?" And he looked at me and quietly said, "You had no choice. You're what you had to be."

NF: Toni Cade Bambara said, "The job of the writer is to make revolution irresistible."

LC: Well—I can understand that. Revolution has to be very widely defined. When people read that, some people will say, thinking narrowly, Oh she's trying to get people to fight. But there was a time when I was very jealous—I wouldn't act like it, of course—of June Jordan. June was tough, let me tell you. June would hit you in the mouth. Tough. But see June wasn't like that. June and I were two weeks apart in age. But I used to think, "Why can't I write like that? I want to write like June." Then it occurred to me. People used to say I was strong, strong in my work. I used to say, "What's strong about me?" But now, yes, I do think some of the things might be revolutionary. I have come to think this is so as

I enter my seventieth year. Because I just think that we define "revolutionary things" so narrowly. The job of the art, it seems to me, is to not leave you where it found you.

NF: That would be revolutionary indeed.

LC: I was at the Dodge Festival when Amiri [Baraka] read his poem ["Somebody Blew Up America"]. I was there with my friends Michael and Kathy. He's Jewish and she's an ex-nun. I'm godmother to their kids. Michael, when he started hearing all of what Amiri was saying, got all worried because he [Michael] said, "I must be a bad Jew." He wasn't offended. There are some words that are easier for some people to hear. I don't think as a poet you should ever make it easier for people, but I think you should think of all the possibilities and then go for it! Everything in our culture, especially now, is geared toward everybody being the same. Looking the same at least. Imagine a place where the schools, the training places, teach, "This is how we act in America, if we're nice."

When I do readings, I talk about my sister Josephine, who was a prostitute. Why wouldn't I talk about her? She was such an interesting woman. Families have all kinds of people in them. This is what is going to be interesting about New Orleans. Interesting and scary. Because New Orleans is not the buildings; it's the people. There is going to be a mistake made in trying to rebuild these buildings and not rebuild and bring back these humans. Preservation is typically about the buildings and not about the people, and the people are what have made New Orleans what it is. I don't understand not thinking about this in this way. Don't you know that when this happens this other is bound to happen? Karma is real. I believe it. I've seen it.

NF: Are you a "quick study," Lucille Clifton?

LC: I used to be. But that was long ago.

NF: At what?

LC: I used to test well. I always tested beyond what I really knew. If I've heard something once it's still there. I was on *Jeopardy!* a few times actually.

NF: The television game show?

LC: Oh yes [*laughs*]! When Art Fleming was the host, I was a five-time winner. You didn't know this?

NF: I had no idea.

LC: Oh, they were just so tickled. They were all shocked because here was this colored girl winning *Jeopardy!* back in the 1960s. My daughter Gilly had just been born. She's now forty-two. Long time ago. Then I came back on when Alex Trebek came on as host, and I must explain what happened. I didn't have my bifocals on. I couldn't see a thing. Everything about the old show had changed. You had to first see the light before you hit the buzzer, and I couldn't see anything. There were all these different categories. It used to be much harder than it is now. I had overheard or heard so many different things in my life because I'm interested in so many different kinds of things. I could just remember these things so sharply. I know a lot about everything that doesn't matter. I truly do [*laughs*].

NF: I am going to find this tape and watch you.

LC: Oh, please, and let me see it if you do. Yes. Five days in a row I was there. I was so thin. You'd never recognize me.

NF: Yes I would. You would be the woman with the ringing ears [*laughs*]. May I have permission to give Lucille Clifton a writing exercise?

LC: Oh Lord, I have to get pen and paper and write something?

NF: No. We both are primarily oral, so let's "write it" that way. This is an exercise called "Charm." Think of a moment in your life so precious that if you could wear it you would. A moment, so divine. What would it—

LC: A photograph. My mother. So clear. She was a large woman with wild hair. She—even now—in my other life I am halfway psychic—she has protected my children and watched over them. She died a month before my oldest daughter was born and that left me in such disarray. That is the photograph I always wear. It's never away from me. It's forty-seven years away from me. It's as sharp as ever. And now my husband is dead. I have two children who are dead. My brother is dead. I have had many losses. I don't really understand it all. I plan to talk to the deities about it. I plan to talk to Zeus, whoever? Because I don't understand it and I want to. But my mother would absolutely be my sacred thing to wear.

NF: Who are the members of your tribe?

LC: Oh my, what an interesting question. My tribe . . . my ultimate tribe would probably be poetry people. It's a mixed bag of people though. I might be one of the few people who live in all the worlds of poetry. There are so many Black poets who live only in the Black world. I do a lot of introducing of people. That's my thing. At the Dodge Festival. "Look here Maxine this is so-and-so. . . ." Just thinking that of course you want to know this person. They do what you do. They feel what you feel. They understand in the way that you do. And then there are mothers. That's certainly my tribe. They are definitely my tribe. Mothering is what I thought I knew how to do but still I lost two children. The tribe of mystics maybe? I know a little something about mysticism. I incorporate it into my life and work. That doesn't mean I have to go around looking weird. Poets tend to be my tribe. But none of them exactly. Most poets now are people in graduate schools. I've never been a person who has been overtaught. Though I like smart folks. My husband was a very intellectual man. Fred was one of the planners of the African American Studies Department at Harvard. He taught at Harvard.

NF: Why do you use lowercase in your poems?

LC: I like the look of it. I like the way it looks all of one piece. Right now I'm learning to write on a computer. I've always worked on a video writer. They don't make the disks anymore. There's one right now on eBay, but maybe not anymore. I'm working on Microsoft now, or trying to. I'm trying to learn to make the computer not capitalize the beginning of every line. People are always saying, "Oh Lucille, you must think more of yourself," and I say, "Excuse me . . . I think very highly of myself . . . some days . . . and some days I don't" [*laughs*].

NF: So, it's a visual thing?

LC: Absolutely a visual thing. I think of the poem as a whole thing.

NF: Your poetry confronts chaos, lost love, disorder, violence, pain. You incorporate such wit, humor, lament, storytelling, and always transcendence. Are you a blues singer?

LC: No [*laughs*]. But I love the blues. And you know something? I sing all the time. I hum all the time when I'm in the classroom and I rock (side to side) and I don't think the students notice, but maybe they do. When I'm writing, I try to write to music. I use music. Which music depends on how I feel. My mother knew Sarah Ward. Mahalia Jackson and another Black woman singer who used to come through Buffalo used to stay with us. In Buffalo in those days, you couldn't stay in any hotel if you were Black, so those that came through used to stay at my grandmother's house. I've been so, so lucky—the people I have met in my life. It's been an interesting—and some days, I think, a tragic—life. But it has been an amazing life in terms of meeting people along the way.

Sometimes we would go to visit my oldest sister, Josephine, in the brothel. My mother thought it was so terrible. People would ask, "Jo, why do they come and see you?" And she would say, "Because we are family." Family meant so much to us. We were taught family is what you've got. All my father's daughters loved crossword puzzles, including me. Josephine would be the prostitute standing on the corner, waiting for a john with a crossword-puzzle book in her hand, saying to the car that just pulled up, "Oh, OK. Just a minute, I'll be right with you. . . ." Yes! She was quite something. Telling her story would be so interesting. When she and her pimp, Dick, heard I was going to Howard, they took me to a restaurant and gave me a list of places where they better not hear that I was hanging around. And they did not hear because I did not go. I don't think we have family like we used to; people talking about the day, talking about our lives. My kids think people are afraid of their children and that they want to be their friend. My girls and I are very close friends but they know who is the mother—it's me [*laughs*]! My husband died of lung cancer. My son smokes but he will not smoke in front of me to this day. And he's "the family dude." It's a kind of respect. Josephine was a little thing. She took care of my father when he was dying. She moved back home and took care of him until the end. Family.

NF: You are an incredibly curious human being. Has your curiosity ever let you down? Have you ever followed it too far?

LC: There are some who would say I always follow it too far! . . . I don't think my curiosity has let me down. I think things have added to me, added to my knowledge about things. My memory has been sure. Sometimes I've learned more than I've wished to. What I wish and what is better are two different things. People have no idea what my life is like. The number of manuscripts that I am sent is so staggering. I am always wondering where is this life going to go next? For instance, once I was in the toilet at the Dodge Festival, and somebody reached under the door and handed me a piece of paper and said, "Can you sign this for me Miss Clifton?" I didn't see who it was, but later I met the person. She was bragging about it. I thought it was the strangest thing. So peculiar. Why would you not think that was an intrusion? And then there are the wonderful things. A friend who was researching some soldiers. I've forgotten which war it was. This one dead soldier . . . soldiers always have things in their pockets when their bodies are found. One of the soldiers had a poem of mine in his pocket. That was really touching to me.

NF: When I read your work sometimes, I hear the voice of a woman who loves to laugh even when the subject is four-star serious.

LC: Laughter is healing. Our laughter might be diminishing a bit in our families. As Black people we see the irony in things so often. Lord, just suppose we couldn't. But the things that are going on among our families; our older people who are not schooled . . . we overestimate the value of school. School is good. But on the other hand, all it is is school. The stories of our folk, laughing at things that are funny, I think that has sustained us. I love Tom Joyner. J. Anthony Brown is a funny guy. Funny. We are able to sustain ourselves. I am well aware, have heard many times that I am not Black enough. Well—I'm as Black as I can be. And I have also heard that I do not value what our struggle has been. I know exactly what our struggle has been. I've been involved in some of our struggle. But—I have to keep myself human and that's something beyond some of those other things that people want me to be first. I know how people would like me to sound. I know and I get put out about it sometimes. One of my dearest friends is Sonia [Sanchez]. Sonia thinks my work is as well known among Black people as her work. Of course it's not. That's my girl though. But my other *girl* is Sharon, Sharon Olds. These are not people who are very much like each other. But they are in the same tribe. They are.

NF: Any unsung names you might like to call?

LC: I'm well aware, I try to remain aware . . . that somewhere in some little city is a woman and she can outwrite me hands down and nobody knows her name and she just needs a chance. I think that's very important to remember. It's important for me to remember. My whole life to me has been a shock. I never attempted to get published because I didn't know you could, and at that time somebody who looked like me couldn't.

NF: You are so many different things. Forgive me for bringing out the label gun, but what about you might be southern?

LC: I believe I have a southern way of intuiting in the world. Storytelling, which my folks always did. Just a way of trying to understand and of bearing things, even though I'm tired of doing it right now, I know how to bear things. I try to be kind. I try not to be judgmental. Maybe there is a certain desire to not make waves when you are raised in the South. But I kind of like to make waves myself. Not to say anything about stuff never seemed to be helpful. To notice things is also southern. To notice everything. The way we have had to live in the world is to pretend to not pay attention, but I love history. All of it. Not just the part that is interesting. I teach a course at St. Mary's College called Unpopular American History. I can talk about race and not be nervous about it. In the North still in many places when you are Black and walk into a room filled with Whites, the feeling is quite often, "What are you doing here?" In the South when you are Black and walk into a room of White people the look is quite often, "Oh, you're here, of course, but what are you doing?"

NF: I've witnessed and been a part of audiences rising from their chairs after the introduction of merely your name being set loose into the air. Standing ovations before any poem is ever read. How does being given that honor feel to *An Ordinary Woman*?

LC: Oh dear [*laughs*]. Confusing. I don't know. I'm tickled. Of course I'm tickled. And then there's the fear of "Wait till I read these words. They'll all start walking out." It is a wonderful tribute. I'm not as good as they think I am. I'm not as nice as they think I am, but what the heck.

I try to be an honorable person. I try to face life with grace and courage. I'm scared of lightning, among other things, mice and rats, both of them I know quite well, growing up where I grew up. I lived in a wonderful home on the Chesapeake Bay and in the projects, so I know a whole gamut of worlds. The first time that standing-up thing happened was at the Dodge Festival. I said, "Wow, what am I getting ready to say? It's not good enough whatever it will be." And then I thought, "Maybe they think I'm my sister Elaine" [*laughs*]. I'm trying to be an honorable person. Trying my best to be.

Shirlette Ammons: "History Makes Concessions for White Boys" and "apathy no more" first appeared in *Stumphole: Aunthology of Bakwoods Blood*, Big Drum Press, Chapel Hill, North Carolina.

Houston Baker Jr.: "Another Man" and "In the Break" reprinted from *Blues Journeys Home: New and Selected Poems* with the permission of the author, published by Lotus, Detroit, Michigan, 1985.

Holly Bass: "seven crown man" appeared in *nocturnes (re)view* and *Cave Canem X.*

Remica L. Bingham: "Simmie Knox Paints Bill Clinton for the White House" and "O'Connor's South" © 2007 by Remica L. Bingham, reprinted from *Conversion* with permission of Lotus Press, Detroit, Michigan.

Earl Braggs: "Storm Named Earl" and "Of Course the Brochure Doesn't Mention Mrs. Abbott" first appeared in *Crossing Tecumseh Street*, published by Anhinga Press, Tallahassee, Florida.

Jericho Brown: "Like Father" first appeared in *Callaloo.*

Gloria Burgess: "Sanctuary" © 2001 by Gloria Burgess, first published in *Colors Northwest Magazine*, reprinted from *The Open Door*, published by Red Oak Press, Edmonds, Washington.

Jarvis Q. DeBerry: "Juke Joint Josephine" © 2001 by Jarvis Q. DeBerry, reprinted from *Gathering Ground: A Reader Celebrating Cave Canem's First Decade* with the permission of the author.

Ronald Dorris: "St. Philip Blues" first appeared in *Cave Canem V.*

Camille T. Dungy: "Dinah in the Box" previously appeared in *Mid-American Review* and *From the Fishouse*. "Farm Bureau Advisor" © 2006 by Camille T. Dungy, reprinted from *What to Eat, What to Drink, What to Leave for Poison* with the permission of Red Hen Press, Los Angeles, California.

CONTRIBUTORS

Shirlette Ammons is a poet, writer, and musician, who also directs an arts program for children. Her first collection of poetry, entitled *Stumphole Anthology of Bakwoods Blood*, was published in September 2002. She is also vocalist and cobassist for her band, mosadi music, whose debut album was released in 2006. Her poetry and essays have appeared in *Asheville Review, Fierce Magazine, Independent Weekly, Venus Magazine*, and other publications. She has received the Kathryn H. Wallace Award for Artists in Community Service and the United Arts Council Emerging Artist Grant for songwriting. Shirlette resides in Durham, North Carolina, with her partner and their dog, Zaji.

Askhari overdoses on activism (not altruism), sports, sunrises, and other things aggressive. Recently, she has given up looking for money under sofa cushions and trying to save the world. Now, she has more time available to eat watermelon, watch 24, listen to Nina Simone and Rick James, and play Taboo. Her work has appeared in *Essence, Black Issues Book Review, Class, Catalyst, Rappages, Urban Profile, In the Tradition, Testimony, Sex, and the Single Girl*, and *Role Call: A Generational Anthology of Social and Political Black Art and Literature.*

Alvin Aubert's poetry collections are *Against the Blues, Feeling Through, South Louisiana, If Winter Come, Harlem Wrestler,* and *The Way I Do.* He is the founding editor of the literary journal *Obsidian* and is the recipient of two National Endowment for the Arts awards for his poetry, which has also appeared, in addition to several articles and reviews, in various periodicals. He is a Wayne State University professor emeritus and now lives in retirement near Princeton University with his librarian wife, Bernadine.

Houston Baker Jr. is a native of Louisville, Kentucky. He received his BA (magna cum laude and Phi Beta Kappa) from Howard University and his MA and PhD degrees from UCLA. He has taught at Yale, the University of Virginia, and the University of Pennsylvania. Currently, he is the Susan Fox and George D. Beischer Professor of English at Duke University. He is the editor of *American Literature*, the oldest and most prestigious journal in American Literary Studies. Professor Baker began his career as a scholar of British Victorian literature but made a shift to the study of Afro-American literature and culture. He has published or edited more than twenty books and is the author of more than eighty articles, essays, and reviews. His most recent books include *Turning South Again: Re-Thinking Modernism / Re-Reading Booker T.* and *Critical Memory: Public Spheres, African American Writing, and Black Fathers and Sons in America*. He is also a published poet whose most recent title is *Passing Over*. He has served in a number of administrative and institutional posts, including the 1992 presidency of the Modern Language Association of America. His honors include Guggenheim, John Hay Whitney, and Rockefeller Fellowships, as well as eleven honorary degrees from American colleges and universities.

Holly Bass, a writer and performer, has presented her work at respected regional theaters and performance spaces such as Arena Stage, Woolly Mammoth Theater, the Athenaeum Theatre, the Kennedy Center, the Whitney Museum, and the Experience Music Project. She has received two Artist Fellowship grants from the D.C. Commission on the Arts and Humanities. She is a Cave Canem fellow, and her poems have appeared in *Callaloo, Nocturnes (Re)view of the Literary Arts*, and *Role Call*. Her essay on women and hip-hop theater appears in the contemporary feminist anthology *The Fire This Time: Young Activists and the New Feminism*. She studied modern dance (under Viola Farber) and creative writing at Sarah Lawrence College before earning an MA in Journalism from Columbia University.

Remica L. Bingham received her MFA from Bennington College. She has attended the Callaloo Creative Writing Workshops and is a Cave Canem fellow. She is the recipient of the 2005 Hughes, Diop, Knight Poetry Award and was nominated for a 2005 Pushcart Prize. Her first book of poetry, *Conversion*, won the 2006 Naomi Long Madgett Poetry Award and will be published by Lotus Press in 2007. Currently, she is the Writing Competency Coordinator at Norfolk State University in Norfolk, Virginia.

Earl Braggs, a professor of English, teaches writing and literature at the University of Tennessee at Chattanooga. He is the author of five collections of poetry, including *Crossing Tecumseh Street, House on Fontanka, Walking Back from Woodstock, Hats*, and *Hat Dance Blue* (winner of the 1992 Anhinga Prize). His latest collection, *In Which Language Do I Keep Silent?* is scheduled for publication in 2006. In addition to poetry, Braggs also writes fiction, for which he was awarded the 1995 Jack Kerouac Literary Prize.

Jericho Brown holds the C. Glen Cambor Fellowship at the University of Houston, where he is a PhD student in literature and creative writing. His poems have appeared in *Bloom, Callaloo, Indiana Review,* and *Prairie Schooner*. He is also the recipient of the 2006 Michener Fellowship and serves as poetry editor at *Gulf Coast: A Journal of Literature and Fine Arts.*

Gloria Burgess's poetry celebrates the oral traditions of her ancestors—African and Native American. Her poetry books include *The Open Door* and *Journey of the Rose*. She has also written a book about her father's life-changing relationship with William Faulkner and is the author of *Legacy Living: The Six Covenants for Personal and Professional Excellence*, an inviting tapestry of poetry, art, and inquiry, providing guidance on living a life of service. Dr. Burgess lives in the Pacific Northwest.

Christian Campbell, of the Bahamas and Trinidad and Tobago, is a poet, cultural critic, and journalist. He read English at Balliol College, University of Oxford as the 2002 Commonwealth Caribbean Rhodes Scholar, and is nearing completion of a PhD in English at Duke University. Sonia Sanchez recently named his manuscript, *Running the Dusk*, one of two honorable mention finalists for the Cave Canem Poetry Prize.

Robin Caudell was born and raised on Maryland's eastern shore. She holds a BS in Journalism from the University of Maryland at College Park and an MFA in Writing from Goddard College. She lives and works in the Adirondack / Lake Champlain region of New York. Currently, she is researching nineteenth-century Africans in America and commemorating her ancestors in her haibun, "Black Heel Strings: A Tidewater Memoir."

Lucille Clifton was born in Depew, New York, in 1936. Her books of poetry include *Mercy; Blessing the Boats: New and Selected Poems 1988–2000*, which won the National Book Award; *The Terrible Stories*, which was nominated for the National Book Award; *The Book of Light; Quilting: Poems 1987–1990; Next: New Poems; Good Woman: Poems and a Memoir 1969–1980*, which was nominated for the Pulitzer Prize; *Two-Headed Woman*, also a Pulitzer Prize nominee and winner of the University of Massachusetts Press Juniper Prize; *An Ordinary Woman; Good News about the Earth;* and *Good Times*. She has also written *Generations: A Memoir* and more than sixteen books for children. Her honors include an Emmy Award from the American Academy of Television Arts and Sciences, a Lannan Literary Award, two fellowships from the National Endowment for the Arts, the Shelley Memorial Award, and the YM-YWHA Poetry Center Discovery Award. In 1999 she was elected a chancellor of the Academy of American Poets. She has served as poet laureate for the state of Maryland and is currently professor emeritus at St. Mary's College of Maryland.

Taiyon Coleman is a member of Cave Canem, and her work has appeared in *Ethos, Knotgrass, Sketch, Drumvoices Revue, Sauti Mpya, Words Will Heal the Wound: A Celebration of Community Through Poetry* (CD Volume II), *Bum Rush the Page, A View from the Loft*, and *Maverick Magazine #9*.

Lauri Conner is a poet and writer working and living in Seattle. Her work has appeared in the *Seattle Review, Calyx, Gathering Ground: A Reader Celebrating Cave Canem's First Decade*, and other journals and anthologies. She teaches creative writing at Seattle Academy and is working on her PhD in language, literacy, and culture.

Jane Alberdeston Coralín's work has been published in *Louisiana Literature*, the *Paterson Literary Review, Bilingual Review, Step into a World: A Global Anthology of the New Black Literature, Bum Rush the Page, Black Issues Book Review*, and other anthologies and journals. She received the 2004 Associated Writing Program's Intro Journals Award. Jane cowrote *Sister Chicas: A Novel*, released by Penguin Books/New American Library in early 2006. Currently a doctoral student at SUNY Binghamton, she is working on a novel based on her great-grandfather's migration from Guadeloupe to Puerto Rico. Jane is also a proud alumna of Cave Canem.

Matilda Cox is currently an advisor and administrator at Old Dominion University where she received her MA in English. She also occasionally teaches classes in writing and literature. She has always written poetry and has been published in literary magazines and in *Turnings: An Anthology of Women's Writing*.

Curtis Crisler is a limited-term lecturer at Indiana Purdue Fort Wayne (IPFW). He has a forthcoming book from Front Street Press entitled *Tough Boy Sonatas*. A Cave Canem fellow, he has recently published in *Elixir, Reverb, L'intrigue: Nature Anthology, The Fourth River, Only the Sea Keeps: Poetry of the Tsunami*, and *Attic*.

DeLana Dameron was born and raised in Columbia, South Carolina. Currently a senior at the University of North Carolina at Chapel Hill, she studies African and Middle Eastern history and meddles in several creative writing courses, forever trying to marry the historical and the literary. She has been featured in venues associated with the university and the surrounding community and is a member of the Carolina African American Writers' Collective.

Traci Dant holds an MFA in Creative Writing from Washington University in St. Louis. She has received fellowships from the MacDowell Colony, the Cave Canem Foundation, and the Illinois Arts Council. Her poetry has been published in *Crab Orchard Review, PoemMemoirStory:* PMS, and *Gathering Ground*. She lives in Aurora, Illinois, with her husband and son.

Jarvis Q. DeBerry was raised in Mississippi where poetry played a central role. Every church occasion required small children and sometimes adults to recite the poems they had memorized. Jarvis's maternal grandmother, however, made it clear that poems could live outside the church and outside the volumes in which they were bound. A storehouse of poems by Paul Laurence Dunbar and James Weldon Johnson, she instilled in her grandson a love of poems both practical and accessible.

Ronald Dorris is a lifelong resident of Garyville, Louisiana, a small sugarcane town thirty-five miles west of New Orleans. His poetry and prose have appeared in *Quarterly West, Western Humanities Review, Genetic Dancer, The Griot, American Poetry Anthology, Obsidian II, Cave Canem, Louisiana English Journal, Xavier Review, Langston Hughes Colloquy,* and *Network 2000: In the Spirit of the Harlem Renaissance.*

Mitchell L. H. Douglas, a native of Louisville, Kentucky, is an assistant professor of creative writing at Indiana University–Purdue University Indianapolis. A founding member of the Affrilachian Poets, he earned an MFA in poetry from Indiana University Bloomington where he was a Booth Tarkington Fellow and an associate poetry editor for the *Indiana Review*. His poetry has appeared in *Callaloo* and the Gival Press anthology *Poetic Voices Without Borders.*

Camille T. Dungy, author of *What to Eat, What to Drink, and What to Leave for Poison* (Red Hen Press, 2006), has received fellowships and awards from organizations including the National Endowment for the Arts, the Virginia Commission for the Arts, Cave Canem, the American Antiquarian Society, and the Bread Loaf Writers' Conference. Dungy currently lives in San Francisco, California, where she serves as an associate professor in the Creative Writing Department at San Francisco State University.

Cornelius Eady is the author of six books of poetry: *Kartunes* (Warthog Press, 1980); *Victims of the Latest Dance Craze* (Ommation Press, 1986), winner of the 1985 Lamont Prize from the Academy of American Poets; *The Gathering of My Name* (Carnegie Mellon University Press, 1991), nominated for the 1992 Pulitzer Prize in Poetry; *You Don't Miss Your Water* (Henry Holt and Co., 1995); *Autobiography of a Jukebox* (Carnegie Mellon University Press, 1997); and *Brutal Imagination* (Putnam, 2001). He is the recipient of an NEA Fellowship in Literature (1985), a John Simon Guggenheim Fellowship in Poetry (1993), a Lila Wallace–Reader's Digest Traveling Scholarship to Tougaloo College in Mississippi (1992–1993), a Rockefeller Foundation Fellowship to Bellagio, Italy (1993), and the Prairie Schooner Strousse Award (1994). His work appears in many journals and magazines and in the anthologies *Every Shut Eye Ain't Asleep*, *In Search of Color Everywhere*, and *The Vintage Book of African American Poetry*. In June 1997, an adaptation of *You Don't Miss Your Water* was performed at the Vineyard Theatre in New York City. In 1999, *Running Man*, a musical theater piece cowritten with jazz musician Diedre Murray, was a finalist for the Pulitzer Prize in Drama and won Obie Awards for best musical score and best lead actor in a musical. In January 2002, a production of *Brutal Imagination* (with a score by Diedre Murray) opened at the Vineyard Theatre and won the 2002 Oppenheimer award for the best first play by an American playwright. Eady has taught poetry at SUNY Stony Brook, where he directed its Poetry Center, City College, Sarah Lawrence College, New York University, the Writer's Voice, the 92nd St Y, the College of William and Mary, and Sweet Briar College. With poet Toi Derricotte, he is cofounder of Cave Canem. At present he is an associate professor of English and director of the Creative Writing Program at the University of Notre Dame.

Teri Elam-Blanchard currently lives and writes poetry, happily, inside the city limits of Atlanta. She has credits in various magazines and books, and in her spare time, she also photographs poets.

Zetta Elliott, Canadian by birth, has spent the past twelve years writing, teaching, and studying in the United States. One of her poems, "Played Out," has been published in *Coloring Book: An Eclectic Anthology of Fiction and Poetry by Multicultural Writers*, and her novella, *Plastique*, was excerpted in *T Dot Griots:*

An Anthology of Toronto's Black Storytellers. Her essays have been published in *Black Arts Quarterly* and *WarpLand.*

Kelly Norman Ellis is an associate professor of English and creative writing at Chicago State University. Her work has appeared in *Sisterfire, Spirit and Flame, Calyx, Obsidian II, Cornbread Nation, WarpLand, Boomer Girls, Role Call,* and *Essence.* Her first collection of poetry, *Tougaloo Blues* (Third World Press), was published in 2003. She is a founding member of the Affrilachian Poets and a Cave Canem fellow.

Thomas Sayers Ellis was born and raised in Washington, D.C. He cofounded the Dark Room Collective and received his MFA from Brown University in 1995. His work has appeared in *American Poetry Review, Best American Poetry* (1997 and 2001), *Callaloo, Fence, Grand Street, Hambone, Harvard Review, Kenyon Review, Ploughshares, Pushcart Prize* (1998), and *Giant Steps: The New Generation of African American Writers.* He has received fellowships from the MacDowell Colony and the Fine Arts Work Center, among others. Mr. Ellis is a contributing editor of *Callaloo,* and his first collection, *The Good Junk,* was published in the Graywolf annual *Take Three.* He is also the author of *The Maverick Room,* a chapbook entitled *The Genuine Negro Hero,* and the forthcoming chaplet *Song On.* An associate professor of English at Case Western Reserve University and a faculty member of the Lesley University low-residency MFA program, his *We Miracles: Notes for Black Poets* is also forthcoming from the University of Michigan Press.

jaye farren has not always wanted to be a writer. In fact, she envisioned herself selling paintings out of a tiny home studio or sketching portraits on the streets of Paris. Even though she scribbled a few poems and typed out a short story or two, it wasn't until jaye turned twenty that she began writing seriously, inspired by the likes of Audre Lorde, Jayne Cortez, Gabriel García Márquez, Alice Walker, and Neil Gaiman. jaye farren hopes to continue making art until death shows up with a pair of glue-on wings.

Chanda Feldman grew up in Tennessee. She received an MFA in poetry from Cornell University and a BA in English literature from the University of Chicago. Chanda is a Cave Canem fellow and the recipient of scholarships from the Squaw Valley Writers' Conference and the Walker Foundation for the Provincetown Center for the Arts summer workshops. Her poems have recently appeared or are forthcoming in *Bellingham Review, The Journal, Poetry Northwest,* and *Spoon River Poetry Review.* She lives in San Francisco.

Reginald Flood lives in a small town in southeastern Connecticut. He has an MA in literature and creative writing from Syracuse University, and a PhD in British and American literature and culture from the University of Southern California. "Poem for June Jordan" is from a manuscript he is working on entitled *Dancing on the Master's Table*. He teaches in the English Department at Eastern Connecticut State University.

Cherryl Floyd-Miller is the 2006 winner of the Poetry Daily–Virginia Arts of the Book Companion Poems Contest. She has published two volumes of poetry, *Utterance: A Museology of Kin* (2003) and *Chops* (Nexus Press, 2004). Her poems have appeared in *Poetry* magazine, *Crab Orchard Review*, *Terminus*, *Copper Nickel*, and *StorySouth*. She has received grants and fellowships from Poets & Writers, Inc., Idyllwild Summer in Poetry, Caldera, the Fulton County Arts Council, Cave Canem, and the Vermont Studio Center. She is also a quilt artist and teaches creative writing to adults in her community.

Joanne Gabbin is a professor of English at James Madison University where she is the executive director of the Furious Flower Poetry Center. She is author of *Sterling A. Brown: Building the Black Aesthetic Tradition*, editor of *Furious Flower: A Revolution in African American Poetry* and *The Furious Flowering of African American Poetry*, and executive producer of the Furious Flower video and DVD series. A dedicated teacher and scholar, she has received numerous awards for excellence in teaching and scholarship.

Christopher Gilbert lives in Providence, Rhode Island. He is a past winner of the Walt Whitman Award given by the Academy of American Poets and is a recipient of NEA fellowships in poetry writing. Gilbert teaches psychology at Bristol Community College in Fall River, Massachusetts.

Nikki Giovanni was born in Knoxville, Tennessee, and raised in Ohio. In 1960, she entered Fisk University, where she worked with the school's Writer's Workshop and edited the literary magazine. After receiving her BA, she organized the Black Arts Festival in Cincinnati and then entered graduate school at the University of Pennsylvania. In her first two collections, *Black Feeling, Black Talk* and *Black Judgment*, Giovanni reflects on African American identity. Recently, she has published *The Collected Poetry of Nikki Giovanni*, *Quilting the Black-Eyed Pea: Poems and Not Quite Poems*, *Blues for All the Changes: New Poems*, *Love Poems*, and *Selected Poems of Nikki Giovanni*. Her honors include the NAACP Image Award for Literature and the Langston Hughes Award for Distinguished Contributions to Arts and Letters. Several magazines have named

Giovanni Woman of the Year, including *Essence, Mademoiselle,* and *Ladies' Home Journal.* She is currently University Distinguished Professor of English and Gloria D. Smith Professor of Black Studies at Virginia Tech.

Ebony Golden is a community artist and educator who currently resides in Durham, North Carolina. She earned an MFA in poetry from American University and has published poems in *WarpLand* and *Black Arts Quarterly.* Ebony's mission is to empower individuals to pursue creative expression, social change, and divine spirit through the arts. Her first poetry chapbook, *The Sweet Smell of Juju Funk,* was published by her grassroots literary press, Betty's Daughter (April 2006). goldendharma@yahoo.com

Jaki Shelton Green is the 2003 recipient of the North Carolina Award for Literature. Her poetry has appeared in publications such as *The Crucible, African American Review, Obsidian, Poets for Peace, Immigration, Emigration, and Diversity, Ms.,* and *Essence.* Her publications are *Dead on Arrival, Masks, Conjure Blues, Singing a Tree into Dance, Breath of the Song,* and *Blue Opal,* a play. She is the 2006 writer in residence at the Taller Portobelo Summer Art Colony in historic Portobelo, Panama.

Forrest Hamer is the author of *Call and Response* (1995), *Middle Ear* (2000), and *Rift* (2007). He is the winner of the Beatrice Hawley Award from Alice James Books and the Northern California Book Award. He has received fellowships from the California Arts Council and the Bread Loaf Writers' Conference and has taught on the poetry faculty at the Callaloo Creative Writing Workshops.

Kendra Hamilton is the author of *The Goddess of Gumbo,* published by Word Press in November 2006. Her work has also been seen in *Callaloo, Shenandoah, Southern Review, River Styx,* and *Obsidian III,* as well as the anthologies *Bum Rush the Page* and *The Best of Callaloo.* One of only twelve southern writers invited to the Spoleto Festival USA's forum on the Confederate flag, Ms. Hamilton has been a fellow both at Cave Canem and at the Rockefeller Foundation's retreat center in Bellagio, Italy.

Duriel E. Harris is a cofounder of the Black Took Collective and a poetry editor for *Obsidian III. Drag* (Elixir Press, 2003), her first book, was hailed by *Black Issues Book Review* as one of the best poetry volumes of the year. A Cave Canem fellow, MacDowell Colony fellow, and member of Douglas Ewart's Inventions jazz orchestra, Harris teaches poetry at Saint Lawrence University in upstate New York.

Reginald Harris's *Ten Tongues* was a finalist for the 2003 Lambda Literary Award and the *ForeWord* Book of the Year Award. Recipient of Individual Artist Awards for both Poetry and Fiction from the Maryland State Arts Council, his work has appeared in numerous venues, including *African American Review*, *Gargoyle*, *Poetry Midwest*, *Sou'wester*, and the *Role Call*, *Bum Rush the Page*, and *Gathering Ground* anthologies.

Vida Henderson is from New Iberia, Louisiana. She currently works as a pharmacist and business owner in New Orleans. A graduate of Cave Canem, she is currently pursuing an MFA in creative writing at Queens University of Charlotte.

Niki Herd graduated from Antioch University Los Angeles. Her work has appeared in *Kalliope*, *Poemmemoirstory: PMS*, *Black Issues Book Review*, and *Xcp: Cross-Cultural Politics*. She is a Cave Canem fellow.

Sean Hill, a native of Milledgeville, Georgia, is a Cave Canem fellow. His poems have appeared in literary journals including *Callaloo*, *Indiana Review*, *Pleiades*, and *Ploughshares*, and in the anthologies *Blues Poems* and *Gathering Ground*. Among his honors and awards are scholarships to the Bread Loaf Writers' Conference, a fellowship to the MacDowell Colony, and a Bush Artist Fellowship.

Lita Hooper is a poet, playwright, and photographer who lives in Atlanta, Georgia. She is an associate professor of English at Georgia Perimeter College and the founding member of the Baobab Poetry Collective. She contributes regularly to anthologies and literary journals. Her most recent collection is *Poetic Revision: The Narrative of Sojourner Truth*. She has also participated in various writers' workshops, including Cave Canem, Hurston-Wright, and Callaloo. Her study of Haki Madhubuti, *The Art of Work: The Art and Life of Haki Madhubuti*, was released in 2006.

Randall Horton, originally from Birmingham, Alabama, currently resides in Chicago, Illinois. He has an MFA in creative writing from Chicago State University. His most recent poems appear in *Dance the Guns to Silence* and *Versal*. He is a coeditor of the upcoming anthology *Fingernails Across the Chalkboard*.

Quentin Huff is an attorney, writer, visual artist, and professional tennis player who lives and works in Winston-Salem, North Carolina. Quentin is a staff writer for PopMatters.com, and his poems have appeared in magazines such as *Defenestration*, *Pemmican Press*, *Poems Nierderngasse*, and *Wicked Alice*. Additionally, Quentin's family owns and operates Huff Art Studio, an art gallery specializing in fine art, printing, and graphic design.

Linda Susan Jackson is the author of two chapbooks: *Vitelline Blues* and *A History of Beauty*. Most recently her work has appeared in *Gathering Ground, Heliotrope, Los Angeles Review, Rivendell, WarpLand, Brooklyn Review 21* and *Brilliant Corners*, among other journals. Her work has also been featured on the From the Fishouse audio archive (www.fishousepoems.org). Her awards include a three-year fellowship to Cave Canem. She is an assistant professor in the English Department at Medgar Evers College/CUNY, and she lives in Brooklyn.

Paula White Jackson is an award-winning poet from South Plainfield, New Jersey. She is a member of the Carolina African American Writers' Collective and has won two Emerging Artist Fellowships. Her first collection was *Saturday Morning Pancakes*. Her work has appeared in the anthology *Catch the Fire!!! Obsidian II, B. Ma: The Sonia Sanchez Literary Review*, and *Life's Spices from Seasoned Sistahs*. Her nonfiction work has appeared in *FYAH* and *Woman's World* magazine.

Reuben Jackson lives in Washington, D.C., where he works as an archivist with the Smithsonian Institution's Duke Ellington Collection. His poems have been included in fourteen anthologies, several journals, and in a volume of poems entitled *Fingering the Keys* (Gut Punch Press, 1991). Reuben also teaches poetry at the Writer's Center in Bethesda, Maryland.

Suzanne Jackson is a painter whose work as a poet has been supported by the Cave Canem Foundation, the St. Mary's Women's Writing Group, and the International Women's Writing Guild. Books featuring her poetry and paintings are *Animal* and *What I Love*. Jackson's poetry and drawings are included in Cave Canem Anthologies I, II, and IV (1996–1999); *Avatar 25* (1996); *Potomac Review* (Winter 1996); and *In the Valley of the Moon* (IWWG, 1994).

Yvonne Jackson is a poet and professor at Talladega College.

Honorée Fanonne Jeffers, a native southerner, now lives on the prairie where she teaches at the University of Oklahoma. She is the author of three books of poetry: *The Gospel of Barbecue* (Kent State University, 2000), *Outlandish Blues* (Wesleyan University, 2003), and *Red Clay Suite* (Southern Illinois University, 2007). She has received an award from the Rona Jaffe Foundation for her poetry as well as fellowships from the MacDowell Colony and the Bread Loaf Writers' Conference.

Valjeanne Jeffers-Thompson was born in Tuskegee, Alabama. She currently resides in Durham, North Carolina, and is a member of the Carolina African American Writers' Collective. Valjeanne is a graduate of Spelman College and is pursuing an MA in psychology at North Carolina Central University. She writes both poetry and science fiction and has completed a draft of her first novel, *Immortal.*

Brandon D. Johnson was born in Gary, Indiana. A resident of Washington, D.C., he received his JD from the Antioch School of Law and works in information marketing. His honors include the Larry Neal Writers' Competition Award, Cave Canem fellow 1997–1999, and a DCCAH Fellowship Grant. His poetry has appeared in *The Drumming Between Us, Callaloo, Drumvoices Revue, Cabin Fever: Poets at Joaquin Miller's Cabin, Beyond the Frontier,* and *Gathering Ground.* He is the author of *The Strangers Between* and a coauthor of *The Black Rooster Social Inn* and the upcoming *Love's Skin.*

Patricia Johnson, a native of Elk Creek, Virginia, lives and works in Roanoke.

Amanda Johnston, a Cave Canem fellow and Affrilachian poet, has received 2003 and 2004 Kentucky Foundation for Women Artist Enrichment grants and the 2005 Austin International Poetry Festival Christina Sergeyevna Award. Johnston is a member of the Austin Project, is a cofounder of the Gibbous Moon Collective, and is the founding editor of *Torch: Poetry, Prose, and Short Stories by African American Women,* www.torchpoetry.org.

Meta DuEwa Jones is an assistant professor of English at the University of Texas at Austin, where she teaches courses on jazz performance, visual culture, and formal innovation in American poetry and African American literature. She received her PhD from Stanford University. Her work has appeared in journals such as *Callaloo, Souls,* and *African American Review.* She is currently coeditor (with Cherise Smith) of a special issue on "Visual Culture and Collaboration" for *Callaloo,* expected in 2007. Her forthcoming book is entitled *The Muse is Music: Jazz, Poetry, and Gendered Performance.*

Parneshia Jones is the recipient of the 2001 Gwendolyn Brooks Poetry Award and the 2003 Margaret Walker Short Story Award. Her work has appeared in *WarpLand* and *Limestone: A Journal of Art and Literature.* She has read and conducted poetry and publishing workshops all over the country including

Columbia College, Vanderbilt University, and Northwestern University. Parneshia lives in Chicago and works in publishing.

Douglas Kearney received an MFA in writing at CalArts (2004) where he now teaches. His work has been published in several anthologies including the World Fantasy Award–winning *Dark Matter: Reading the Bones, Bum Rush the Page,* and *Role Call,* and in several journals including *Callaloo, Nocturnes (Re)view of the Literary Arts,* and *Jubilat.* His first collection of poems, *Fear, some,* was released by Red Hen Press in 2006.

M. Nzadi Keita is a first-generation urban northerner. She is a poet, mother of two sons, fiction writer, spouse, Cave Canem alumna, scholar, and teacher. She has received fellowships for poetry from the Leeway Foundation and the Pennsylvania Council on the Arts and for fiction from Yaddo and the Ragdale Foundation. Her work has appeared in *American Poetry Review, Proteus, Beyond the Frontier: African-American Poetry for the Twenty-First Century, Bum Rush the Page, Impossible to Change: Women, Culture, and the Sixties,* and other publications. Keita teaches creative writing and literature at Ursinus College.

Yusef Komunyakaa was born in Bogalusa, Louisiana, in 1947. Komunyakaa's books of poems include the following: *Taboo: The Wishbone Trilogy, Part 1* (2004); *Pleasure Dome: New and Collected Poems, 1975–1999* (2001); *Talking Dirty to the Gods* (2000); *Thieves of Paradise* (1998), a finalist for the National Book Critics Circle Award; *Neon Vernacular: New and Selected Poems, 1977– 1989* (1993), winner of the Pulitzer Prize and the Kingsley Tufts Poetry Award; *Magic City* (1992); *Dien Cai Dau* (1988), winner of the Dark Room Poetry Prize; *I Apologize for the Eyes in My Head* (1986), winner of the San Francisco Poetry Center Award; and *Copacetic* (1984). Komunyakaa is currently a professor and Distinguished Senior Poet at New York University.

Jacqueline Jones LaMon is a poet and writer. She is a graduate of Mount Holyoke College, UCLA School of Law, and Indiana University, where she received her MFA in poetry. A graduate fellow of Cave Canem, her first poetry collection, *Gravity, U.S.A.,* received the Quercus Review Press Poetry Series 2005 Book Award. She teaches creative writing and literature at Adelphi University.

Quraysh Ali Lansana is the director of the Gwendolyn Brooks Center for Black Literature and Creative Writing at Chicago State University where he is also an assistant professor of English and creative writing. He is the author of *They Shall Run: Harriet Tubman Poems* and *Southside Rain* (Third World Press, 2004 and 2000, respectively) and a coeditor of *Role Call* (Third World Press, 2002) and *Dream of a Word: The Tia Chucha Press Poetry Anthology* (Tia Chucha Press, 2006).

Nathaniel Mackey was born in Miami, Florida, in 1947 and grew up, from age four, in California. He is the author of four books of poetry, the most recent of which is *Splay Anthem* (New Directions, 2006). He is also the creator of an ongoing prose composition, *From a Broken Bottle Traces of Perfume Still Emanate*, of which three volumes have been published, most recently *Atet, A.D.* (City Lights, 2001).

Naomi Long Madgett is the author of eight collections of poetry including *Octavia and Other Poems* and *Connected Islands: New and Selected Poems.* Her autobiography, *Pilgrim Journey*, was published in 2006. She has been poet laureate of Detroit since 2001 and is Professor of English Emerita at Eastern Michigan University. She is also the publisher and editor of Lotus Press, Inc., founded in 1972.

Carrie Allen McCray was born in 1913 in Lynchburg, Virginia. A former social worker and teacher (Talladega College), she has read her poetry at the Spoleto Festival and on National Public Radio's *All Things Considered*, among other places. McCray's work includes: *Freedom's Child*, a memoir; "Adjo Min Van," a short story in John A. Williams's *Beyond the Angry Black*; and *Piece of Time*, a chapbook. Her poems have been widely anthologized. She is a cofounder of the South Carolina Writers Workshop and the recipient of the 2002 Lucy Hampton Literary Award.

Colleen J. McElroy, the former editor of the *Seattle Review* and a professor emerita of the University of Washington, has published over fifteen books including *A Long Way From St. Louie: Travel Memoirs, Travelling Music* (poems), *Over the Lip of the World: Among the Storytellers of Madagascar* (nonfiction), and *Sleeping with the Moon* (poems, forthcoming). Winner of the Before Columbus American Book Award, she also has received two Fulbright Fellowships, two NEA Fellowships, and a DuPont Fellowship.

Dante Micheaux is an emerging poet who resides in New York City.

E. Ethelbert Miller is a literary activist, author, and the board chairperson of the Institute for Policy Studies. His latest book is *How We Sleep on the Nights We Don't Make Love.* www.eethelbertmiller.com

David Mills is a 2005–2006 New York Foundation for the Arts fellow in poetry and has also won a BRIO Individual Artist Grant (1993) and a Chicago State University Hughes Poetry Prize (2003). He has recorded his poetry with RCA records, on Steve Coleman's *Black Science* album, and has opened for Chick Corea and Toots Thielmann in Europe, reciting his poetry. He is also featured in Paul Devlin's poetry documentary *SlamNation*. His poetry has appeared in anthologies such as *Nuyorican Aloud* and in journals such as *Obsidian III*. He received a CEC ArtsLink travel writing fellowship to write Holocaust poems and collaborate with visual artists in a display in Poland, and in 2002, he received a Walker Fellowship to the Fine Arts Work Center in Provincetown. He performs a one-person show of Langston Hughes's work and once lived as writer-in-residence in Hughes's house. In addition to writing and performing poetry, he writes book reviews for the *Washington Post, Boston Globe, Village Voice, Rolling Stone,* and *New York Post,* and he works as a playwright. The Julliard School of Drama commissioned and produced a play he wrote on Dr. Martin Luther King Jr., and in 2005, he was commissioned by Urban Stages Theatre to write a play about Frederick Douglass.

Kamilah Aisha Moon is a Cave Canem fellow, a Paumanok Poetry Award semifinalist, and an Emily Dickinson Award Honorable Mention. Her work has been featured or is forthcoming in *Mosaic, Bittersweet, Open City, Bum Rush the Page, WarpLand, Obsidian III, Essence, Bloom,* and *Gathering Ground.* A native of Nashville, Tennessee, she is currently working on the manuscript *She Has a Name.* Moon received her MFA in creative writing from Sarah Lawrence College.

Indigo Moor is a 2003 recipient of Cave Canem's writing fellowship in poetry and winner of the 2005 Vesle Fenstermaker Poetry Prize for Emerging Writers. His manuscript *Tap-Root* will be published in 2007 by Main Street Rag. His work has appeared in the *Xavier Review, LA Review, Mochila Review,* Boston University's *The Comment,* the Pushcart Prize–nominated *Out of the Blue Artists Unite, Poetry Now,* and *Gathering Ground.*

Lenard D. Moore, founder and executive director of the Carolina African American Writers' Collective, has been nominated twice for a Pushcart Prize. He is the author of *Forever Home* (St. Andrews College Press, 1992). His poetry appears in several magazines and in over forty anthologies. Recipient of the Margaret Walker Creative Writing Award (1997), the Haiku Museum of Tokyo Award (2003, 1994, and 1983), and the Sam Ragan Fine Arts Award (2006), he is an assistant professor of English at Mount Olive College, where he directs the MOC Literary Festival.

Opal Moore is the author of *Lot's Daughters*. Her fiction and poetry have appeared in *Callaloo, Connecticut Review, Nocturnes (Re)view of the Literary Arts, Honey, Hush! An Anthology of African American Women's Humor*, and *Homeplaces: Stories of the South by Women Writers*. Moore, a native Chicagoan, is an associate professor of English at Spelman College in Atlanta, Georgia.

Harryette Mullen teaches English and African American studies at UCLA. Her poems, short stories, and essays have been published widely and reprinted in over fifty anthologies. Her poetry is included in *The Norton Anthology of African American Literature* and has been translated into Spanish, French, Polish, Swedish, Turkish, and Bulgarian. She is the author of six poetry books, including *Recyclopedia* (Graywolf Press, 2006), *Blues Baby* (Bucknell, 2002), and *Sleeping with the Dictionary* (University of California, 2002). The latter was a finalist for a National Book Award, a National Book Critics Circle Award, and a Los Angeles Times Book Prize. In 2004 she received a grant from the Foundation for Contemporary Arts, and in 2005 she was awarded a Guggenheim Fellowship.

Rachel Nelson received her BA from Amherst College and her MFA from the University of Michigan. She lives in Ann Arbor and has facilitated poetry workshops in Michigan prisons.

Mendi Obadike's works include the poetry collection *Armor and Flesh*, the Internet opera *The Sour Thunder*, and commissions from the Whitney Museum, Yale University, the New York African Film Festival, and Electronic Arts Intermix. She lived in Tennessee, Georgia, and North Carolina for twenty-two years. She now lives in the New York City metropolitan area with her husband and collaborative partner (Keith Obadike) and teaches at Princeton University.

Cynthia Parker-Ohene is the daughter of Dorothy Beatrice Kelly, the granddaughter of Mae Kelly, and the great-granddaughter of Lucinda Curry, the women for whom the selected poems were written. These women were born from the Virginia soil, up from slavery. Cynthia received her MFA from the Saint Mary's College of California where she was the Chester Aaron Scholar in Creative Excellence.

Hermine Pinson, poet, fiction writer, and performer, is the author of two poetry collections: *Ashe* and *Mama Yetta and Other Poems*. Her fiction and critical essays have appeared in numerous journals. Her latest work, *Changing the*

Changes in Poetry and Song, is a CD produced in collaboration with Yusef Komunyakaa and Estella Conwill Majozo. Pinson is an associate professor at the College of William and Mary.

Pamela Plummer has lived in the South for twenty years and is the author of two volumes of poetry: *Skin of My Palms* (2004) and *Meditation on Ironing Boards and Other Blues* (1994). She is a recipient of the Hughes, Diop, Knight Poetry Award from the Gwendolyn Brooks Center for Black Literature and Creative Writing, and her poetry appears in numerous journals and anthologies. Plummer currently resides in Birmingham, Alabama.

Stephanie Pruitt is a mother, writer, arts educator, and lover of all things chocolate. She was voted 2004 Poet of the Year by *SpokenVizions* magazine. The Nashville, Tennessee, native is a Cave Canem fellow and an Affrilachian Poet. She currently hosts a children's story time and cohosts *Freestyle,* a sociopolitical and cultural commentary radio talk show. Stephanie is an artist-inresidence with the Tennessee Arts Commission.

Sam Ragland, homegrown and tended to in the bluest grass of Kentucky, graduated with a BA in English writing from Western Kentucky University and will pursue graduate study in literature. She has published creative nonfiction in *I to I: Life Writing by Kentucky Feminists* and poetry in *Zephyrus,* Western Kentucky University's undergraduate journal. She is the daughter of Prentis and Valerie, two poems in unified motion, and the sister of one big brother and two younger sisters.

LaVon Rice was born in Louisville, Kentucky, to a Tennessee-born sharecropper father and a farmer's daughter from Springfield, Kentucky. She always longed for the country her parents left (but not in their words, their ways). Poetry is her first language. One of the rare émigrés from the South in her family, she currently makes her home in New Mexico. www.alchemywordstudio.com

J. W. Richardson is a native of Portsmouth, Virginia, and teaches English at Morehouse College in Atlanta, Georgia.

Gwen Triay Samuels is an ESL/Bilingual teacher in the New Jersey public schools and a New Jersey Certified Court Interpreter/Translator. She renewed her dedication to poetry in 1998 and has since been published in the *Paterson Literary Review* and in several volumes of Cave Canem's yearly anthology. Her poetry will soon be published in the anthology of the Walt Whitman Poetry Festival. Gwen is a second-year Cave Canem fellow.

Sonia Sanchez was born Wilsonia Benita Driver on September 9, 1934, in Birmingham, Alabama. She earned a BA in political science from Hunter College in 1955 and did postgraduate work at New York University, studying poetry with Louise Bogan. Sanchez is the author of more than a dozen books of poetry, including: *Shake Loose My Skin: New and Selected Poems*; *Like the Singing Coming off the Drums: Love Poems*; *Does Your House Have Lions?* which was nominated for both the NAACP Image Award and the National Book Critics Circle Award; *Wounded in the House of a Friend*; *Under a Soprano Sky*; *Homegirls and Hand-grenades*, which won an American Book Award; *I've Been a Woman: New and Selected Poems*; *A Blues Book for Blue Black Magical Women*; *Love Poems*; *Liberation Poem*; *We a BaddDDD People*; and *Home Coming*. Sanchez has also lectured at more than five hundred universities and colleges in the United States and abroad. She was the first Presidential Fellow at Temple University, where she began teaching in 1977, and held the Laura Carnell Chair in English there until her retirement in 1999. She lives in Philadelphia.

Cherene Sherrard, born in Los Angeles, is the daughter of Louisiana migrants who carried their southern heritage with them to California. She is an assistant professor of English at the University of Wisconsin-Madison and holds degrees from UCLA and Cornell University. A graduate of the Cave Canem workshops, her fiction, poetry, and literary criticism have appeared in *American Literature, African American Review, Gulf Coast, Crab Orchard Review,* and *Dark Matter II: Reading the Bones.*

Evie Shockley is a southerner by birth and thrives in sunny, humid climates. Her poetry is collected in *The Gorgon Goddess* (2001) and *A Half-Red Sea* (2006), both published by Carolina Wren Press, and her work also appears in numerous journals and anthologies. After nine years in North Carolina, she began her current position as an assistant professor of English at Rutgers University in New Brunswick, New Jersey.

Kevin Simmonds is a writer and musician originally from New Orleans. His writing has appeared in the journals *Massachusetts Review, Poetry,* and *Field* and in the anthology *Gathering Ground,* and his music has been performed throughout the United States, the United Kingdom, Japan, and the Caribbean. Teaching stints and residencies have brought him to the University of California, Berkeley, the Atlantic Center for the Arts, Bennett College, and the Avery Research Center. In 2005–2006 he held a Fulbright Fellowship in Singapore.

Sharan Strange is a native of Orangeburg, South Carolina. Her work has garnered several fellowships, grants, and awards, including the Rona Jaffe Foundation Writer's Award and the Barnard Women Poets Prize for her collection *Ash*. She has contributed poems and essays to numerous journals and anthologies and to museum and gallery exhibitions in New York and Boston. She lives in Atlanta where she teaches at Spelman College.

Sheree Renée Thomas is a Memphian in New York. Her work has appeared in *Callaloo, Mythic, Southern Revival: Deep Magic for Hurricane Relief, Essence, StorySouth, Tinywords, So Long Been Dreaming, Mojo: Conjure Stories*, and *Bum Rush the Page*. Her *Dark Matter* anthologies have been honored with the World Fantasy Award.

Truth Thomas is an emerging musician and poet from Washington, D.C. He has studied creative writing under Tony Medina and E. Ethelbert Miller at Howard University and is currently pursuing an MFA degree in poetry at New England College in New Hampshire. His work has appeared in *African Voices, Art Times, Lorraine and James, WarpLand, X-Magazine*, and other literary journals.

Natasha Trethewey is the author of *Bellocq's Ophelia* and *Domestic Work*, which was selected by Rita Dove as the inaugural winner of the Cave Canem Poetry Prize. Among her many honors are a Guggenheim Fellowship, the Grolier Poetry Prize, and a Pushcart Prize. Her work has been published and anthologized widely, including in *The New Young American Poets*, in Gioia and Kennedy's *Introduction to Literature* and *Introduction to Poetry*, in *The Oxford Anthology of African-American Poetry*, and twice in *The Best American Poetry*. She is an associate professor of creative writing at Emory University.

Lyrae Van Clief-Stefanon's first collection of poems, *Black Swan*, was selected by Marilyn Nelson as winner of the 2001 Cave Canem Poetry Prize. Her work has appeared in *African American Review, Callaloo, Crab Orchard Review, Shenandoah*, and other journals, as well as in the anthologies *Common Wealth, Gathering Ground, Bum Rush the Page*, and *Role Call*. She is an assistant professor of English at Cornell University.

Frank X Walker, a native of Danville, Kentucky, is the author of three collections of poetry: *Affrilachia, Buffalo Dance: The Journey of York*, and *Black Box*. He is a founding member of the Affrilachian Poets and a Cave Canem fellow. He received his MFA from Spalding University and is the recipient of a Lillian

Smith Book Award, the Thomas D. Clark Award for Literary Excellence, and a Lannan Fellowship for Poetry.

Nagueyalti Warren is a Cave Canem fellow and member of the Baobab Poetry Collective. Her work has appeared in *Essence, African American Review*, and *Obsidian II*. Warren completed an MFA at Goddard College and teaches in the African American Studies Department at Emory University in Atlanta, Georgia. She has edited *Temba Tupu! (Walking Naked) The Africana Woman's Poetic Self*, an anthology forthcoming from the Africa World Press.

Treasure Williams, a native of Meridian, Mississippi, is a Memphis-based writer, freelance editor, journalist, emcee, and emerging poet. She is the Memphis editor of *Drumvoices Revue*. Her performance abilities have been showcased on various projects, most recently on the Turner South television network's My South Speaks ad campaign. She received an MFA from the University of Memphis's creative writing program. The selected poem is from her poetry manuscript, *Feeding the Dead*.

Yolanda Wisher, a poet, singer, songwriter, and musician, lives in the Germantown section of Philadelphia. Her family hails from Westmoreland County and the Shenandoah Valley in Virginia. At twenty-three, Wisher was named the first poet laureate of Montgomery County, Pennsylvania, where she was raised. Her work has been published in *Ploughshares, Fences, Chain, Drumvoices Revue, Black Arts Quarterly*, and *Gathering Ground*. Wisher teaches English and mentors young poets at Germantown Friends School.

Kalamu ya Salaam, a New Orleans editor, writer, filmmaker, and teacher, is the director of Listen to the People, New Orleans's oral history project, the moderator of e-Drum, a listserv for Black writers, and a comoderator, with his son Mtume, of Breath of Life, a Black music Web site. Salaam is codirector of Students at the Center, a writing-based program in the New Orleans public school system. His latest book is the anthology *The End of Forever: Post Katrina New Orleans Poetry*.

Al Young, a poet and novelist and currently the poet laureate of California, was born on May 31, 1939, in Ocean Springs, Mississippi. His volumes of poetry include *Heaven: Collected Poems, 1956–1990, The Blues Don't Change: New and Selected Poems, Geography of the Near Past, Some Recent Fiction, The Song Turning Back into Itself*, and *Dancing: Poems*, which won the Joseph Henry Jackson Award. He is the author of the novels *Seduction by Light, Ask Me Now, Sitting*

Pretty, Who Is Angelina? and *Snakes: A Novel*. His memoirs include *Drowning in the Sea of Love: Musical Memoirs*, *Mingus / Mingus: Two Memoirs* (with Janet Coleman), *Kind of Blue: Musical Memoirs*, and *Bodies and Soul: Musical Memoirs*, which won an American Book Award. Young has also served as the editor of a number of books. His work has been anthologized widely and translated into many languages. Among Young's numerous honors and awards are fellowships from the National Endowment for the Arts and the Guggenheim Foundation, a Wallace Stegner Fellowship, and a Fulbright Fellowship. Al Young has lectured in creative writing at a number of colleges and universities. He lives in California.

Kevin Young is the author of four poetry collections, the most recent of which are *Black Maria*, a film noir in verse, and *Jelly Roll: A Blues*, winner of the Paterson Poetry Prize and a finalist for the National Book Award and the *Los Angeles Times* Book Prize. His first book, *Most Way Home*, was a National Poetry Series selection and winner of the John C. Zacharis First Book Award from *Ploughshares*. Young is also the editor of *Giant Steps: The New Generation of African American Writers*, *John Berryman: Selected Poems*, and Everyman's Pocket Poets *Blues Poems* and *Jazz Poems*. Young is currently Atticus Haygood Professor of English and Creative Writing and Curator of the Raymond Danowski Poetry Library at Emory University in Atlanta, Georgia.